Who Is Jesus?

Who Is Jesus?

Darrell W. Johnson

Regent College Publishing
Vancouver, British Columbia

Published 2011 by Regent College Publishing
5800 University Boulevard, Vancouver, BC V6T 2E4 Canada
Web: www.regentpublishing.com
E-mail: info@regentpublishing.com

Regent College Publishing is an imprint of the Regent Bookstore
<www.regentbookstore.com>. Views expressed in works published by Regent College Publishing are those of the author and do not necessarily represent the official position of Regent College <www.regent-college.edu>.

Cataloguing in Publication / Catalogage avant publication
Library and Archives Canada / Bibliothéque et Archives Canada
550, boul. de la Cité, Gatineau QC
Canada K1A ON4
cip@lac-bac.gc.ca
Tel. / Tél.: 819 994-6881 or / ou 866 578-7777
Fax / Téléc.: 819 934-6777
Government of Canada / Gouvernement du Canada
www.collectionscanada.gc.ca

Johnson, Darrell W., 1947-
  Who is Jesus? / Darrell W. Johnson.
Includes bibliographical references.
ISBN 978-1-57383-451-3
1. Jesus Christ--Person and offices--Sermons. I. Title.

BT203.J655 2010   232   C2010-905081-9

Contents

Preface

The chapters that make up this book ask the single most important question any of us can ever ask. An audacious way to begin, I know. But given the answer—or more accurately, the answers—there is no more critical question any human in any era of history can ask than "Who is Jesus?"

I posed the question most recently in a series of sermons I preached for the congregation where I currently serve (First Baptist of Vancouver, British Columbia). I say "most recently," for given how crucial the question is, I have posed it over the past four decades for other congregations where I have preached, in California, Manila, and around the world. I am profoundly grateful for all those who have joined me in the asking. You have been part of the process by which I have been able to hear the answer(s).

I want to thank members of our church who typed up the manuscripts from my increasingly difficult to read handwriting: Carolyn Vanderhide and Gordon Eekman. And I want to thank Evelyn Loewen, a wordsmith of the highest order, for taking what was originally intended for the ear—sermons—and making it more pleasing to the eye—chapters of a book.

Over the years, so many lay leaders (elders and deacons) have worked to make it possible for me to study, write and preach. It is to them, the "behind-the-scenes" servants, that I dedicate this work. Thank you!

May Jesus Himself make Himself real to you in the following pages. In saying that, I have already begun to answer the question, haven't I?

Read on . . .

I

The Lamb of God Who Takes Away the Sin of the World

John 1:19–34

I can think of no more challenging time in history to be a disciple of Jesus than the one in which we are now living. I can think of more frightening times—like the last half of the first century when under the increasingly aggressive rule of Rome, publicly confessing the crucified Jesus meant the real possibility of being crucified yourself. But I can think of no more challenging time, in every sense of the word, to be a disciple of Jesus than right now.

The whole world is going through massive change in every sector of life. Change in the economic order, the scientific order, the technological order, in the demographic order, in the moral order, in the philosophical order. One way of making sense of reality gives way to another and then to another! It feels like change is the only constant.

I can think of no other challenging place to be a disciple of Jesus than in the place we are living. I can think of more dangerous places—other cities of the world where to name the name of Jesus means certain torture or death. But I can think of no more challenging place to be a disciple of Jesus of Nazareth than right here.

So many of our contemporaries have written off "religion" and in writing off "religion" have sadly written off Jesus. What makes it so challenging is that many who have written off Jesus do not know who He is and what they have written off! Oh, they think they know but they do not, and therein lies the challenge. It is one thing to speak of Jesus and His Gospel in a society that has never heard of Him and His good news. It is another thing altogether to speak of Jesus and His Gospel in a society that thinks it has "heard it all before" and has written Him off.

In this most challenging place, at this most challenging time, the most important discipline of discipleship is to keep asking the question, "Who is Jesus?" As the church I serve says, *"We are a community following Jesus with a heart for the city and beyond."* OK, so who is He? Who is this Jesus we are seeking to follow?

Every new change, every new turning point, every new development in our lives poses the question anew. Or, more accurately, in every new circumstance and at every new turning point Jesus Himself poses the question: "Who do you say that I am? In this challenging time and place, who do you say that I am?"

The answer is going to determine the quality and limit of our vision of what ministries can be done in His name in the city.

Introducing Jesus

I want to begin our study turning to John the Baptist. Why him? John the Baptist was a close relative of Jesus, likely a cousin. John the Baptist grew up with Jesus and would have been aware of all the things people were saying about Jesus. John's mother, Elizabeth, would have surely shared with him the conversations she had with Jesus's mother, Mary. She would likely have told John about the day Mary came to visit when both women were pregnant. When Mary came into the house and greeted Elizabeth, John leaped in Elizabeth's womb. Even *in utero* John knew there was something special, unique, life-altering about his cousin.

I want to begin by turning to John the Baptist because, of all the people that ever lived, he had the greatest privilege anyone could ever have. He is rivaled only by the privilege given to two women. One is Mary, the mother of Jesus, the first person to hold Jesus, the person who nursed Jesus, who raised Jesus. And the other is Mary Magdalene, the first person to meet Jesus alive from the grave. But to John the Baptist was granted the privilege of being the first person to formally introduce Jesus to the world! To prepare him for that privilege God led John into the wilderness away from the city, away from all the noise and glitz and hype. Out where he could think more clearly. Out where he could hear and see more clearly. In the wilderness John came to the conviction that his cousin could some-how meet the horrendous needs of the city. As John told the religious leaders when they came to interrogate him—and although he was the prophet foretold by Isaiah—he was not worthy even to stoop down and untie the straps of Jesus's sandals.

As John set out to introduce his cousin to the world, how was he to adequately articulate what he came to understand? How are we? How do we introduce Jesus to our city and in our time? What words or phrases should we use? What titles or names could possibly do justice to Jesus? As hymn writer Issac Watts expressed:

> Join all the glorious names of wisdom, love and power,
>   that ever mortals know, that angels ever bore;
> All are too mean to speak His worth,
>   Too poor to set my Saviour forth."[1]

John the Baptist sees in Jesus One who has existed from all eternity. Although Jesus is born six months after John, Jesus existed long before John was even a dream in Elizabeth's heart. John says: "After me comes a Man who has a higher rank than I, for He existed before me" (John 1:30).

And John the Baptist sees his cousin Jesus as the only begotten Son of God. John sees in Jesus the One who comes from the heart of God the Father and who through His words and deeds reveals the nature and character of the Father. "I myself have seen, and have testified that this is the Son of God" (John 1:34).

And John the Baptist sees in his cousin, Jesus, One who Himself comes to baptize, not in and with water but in and with the Holy Spirit. Therefore John declares: "This is the One who baptizes in the Holy Spirit" (John 1:33).

This is the One who fills and infuses human life with the very life of God!

And John the Baptist sees in his cousin "the Lamb of God who takes away the sin of the world!" (John 1:29). "Behold," he says. "Look," he says. That is John's characteristic posture. He points away from himself to Jesus. It is the characteristic posture of all Christian witness and preaching: Behold! Look!

The Lamb of God who takes away the sin of the world. This title has, for centuries, played a powerful role in the worship life of God's people; we experience the mercy. Leon Morris of Australia was right when he said: "There is something about the expression which does not require explanation before it can appeal to the depths of the heart. In the words themselves there lurks a luminous quality."[2]

"Look, the Lamb of God who takes away the sin of the world."

Understanding the Terms

No one before John used the exact title. It is a strange way to refer to a human being. What does John want us to know about Jesus? What did John have in mind when he used the phrase? What picture stirred in his imagination as he spoke in this way?

There are four terms in the phrase:

- Lamb
- takes away
- sin
- world

I invite you to explore them with me in reverse order:

- world
- sin
- takes away
- Lamb

World . . . sin . . . takes away . . . the Lamb. True, is it not? On the cross the world's sin takes away the Lamb. And then in the brilliant reverse of Gospel, the Lamb takes away the sin of the world!

World

The first term is "world." The Lamb of God takes away the sin of the *world*. The Greek word for "world" is *kosmos*. In using it, the Baptist is announcing the universal scope of Jesus's work as Lamb. His concern is not only the sin of Israel, not only the sin of the church. His concern is also the sin of Rome and Greece and Egypt and Iraq and India and Afghanistan and China and the USA and Canada. He came to deal with the sin of the whole world. He came to do a cosmic work.

And in using the term "world," the Baptist is announcing grace. Amazing grace. For in the Bible, and especially in the fourth Gospel, *kosmos* particularly refers to the whole human order "which exists in enmity against God."[3] In the Bible, *kosmos* stands for human society organizing itself without God. Jesus the Lamb comes for that world, the real world, our world which ignores God and even resists God's rule and God's kingdom. Mercy!

Sin

This leads to the second term, "sin." The Lamb of God who takes away the *sin* of the world. Note that the Baptist uses the singular, not the plural. Although it is true that the Lamb of God takes away the sins of the world, what especially gripped John is the fact that the Lamb is to take away sin itself.

Specific acts labeled "sins" like gossip, stealing, rape, or murder are only symptoms of sin itself—sin viewed categorically as the sinful human condition from which the symptoms emanate. In his helpful book, *Sin: Overcoming the Ultimate Deadly Addiction*, Keith Miller defines the reality behind the word as:

> a basic and all encompassing, self-centeredness, a need to control in order to get what we want, an attitude that colours every relationship, and emasculates the one with God.... Sin is about our apparent inability to say no to our needs to control people, places and things in order to implement our own self-centered desires; ... we may believe in God and love Him a great deal but at the essential level we are in control—or struggle to be.[4]

Ouch! Miller goes on to argue that this self-absorption we call sin is:

> the same elusive underlying dynamic as that in the life of the traditional chemical addict. Sin is the driving dynamic that leads addicts to fasten upon an addictive chemical or behavior that promises to

fulfill their self-centered and often grandiose dreams and to blot out the feelings that threaten to overtake them. Sin is the universal addiction to self that develops when individuals put themselves in the centre of their personal world in a way that leads to abuse of others and self.[5]

"Infection" is another word we might use to describe this dynamic—deadly infection. How we got it, and whether or not we are born with it is beyond the scope of this text, but the fact remains: it is there and it has a hold on everyone on the face of the globe. And here is the tricky thing about this infection: its chief symptom is denial.[6]

And again quoting Keith Miller:

Denial is the chief characteristic of sin, as it is of a traditional addiction; neither addicts nor sinners can see the extent to which their addiction is ruining their own lives or relationships. This makes both chronic addicts and self-absorbed sinners hard to treat. Both are honestly unaware of the disease's effect on them.[7]

Religious sinners are sometimes the hardest to treat for we have devised all kinds of ways to cover up the fact. We use nicer-sounding euphemisms like "mistakes" or "lapses" or "issues" or "oversights" or "struggles" or "dysfunctions." And as a result we miss the joy of the Gospel. Sin is that deeply rooted need to be our own gods, resulting in alienation (from God and others) and bondage (to drives and desires) beneath our dignity, and it inevitably culminates with death.

Takes Away

We press on to the third term, "takes away." The Lamb of God who *takes away* the sin of the world. In what sense? Obviously sin is still around after the coming of the Lamb of God. What is the Baptizer announcing? The verb he uses has two meanings: (1) take up and carry, and (2) carry off.[8] John the Baptist looks at Jesus of Nazareth and sees in Him One who comes to take up the sin of the world, to carry it as His own and to carry it off. In what sense? How? When?

Lamb of God

We come then to the fourth and most important term, "the Lamb of God." What was in John's mind when he chose it? The problem is there are many possibilities.

The Apocalyptic Lamb

Did he have in mind the so-called "apocalyptic lamb"? For many people of John's day, a lamb—especially a many-horned lamb—was a symbol of power and conquest. New Testament scholar Raymond Brown tells us that "in the context of final judgement there appears in Jewish apocalyptic [literature] the figures of a conquering lamb who will destroy evil in the world."[9]

Is the Baptist pointing to Jesus as the champion of God who fights with sin and overcomes it by superior force? If John had this idea in mind it would explain the ferocity in his early preaching. Matthew remembers John preaching this way:

> The axe is already laid at the root of the trees. . . . His winnowing fork is in His hand, and He will thoroughly clear His threshing floor; and He will gather His wheat into the barn, but He will burn up the chaff with unquenchable fire. (Matt. 3:10, 12)

Does John have this warrior lamb in his mind?

The Lamb Led to the Slaughter

Or did John have in mind "the lamb led to the slaughter" spoken of in Isaiah 53? Isaiah 53 has been called the fifth Gospel. I agree.

> Surely our griefs He Himself bore,
> And our sorrows He carried;

> Yet we ourselves esteemed Him stricken,
> Smitten of God, and afflicted.
> But He was pierced through for our transgressions,
> He was crushed for our iniquities;
> The chastening for our well-being fell upon Him,
> And by His scourging we are healed.
> All of us like sheep have gone astray,
> Each of us has turned to his own way;
> But the LORD has caused the iniquity of us all
> To fall on Him. (Isa. 53:4–6)

Right in the middle of Isaiah's song we read: "Like a lamb that is led to slaughter, and like a sheep that is silent before its shearers" (53:7). Is John saying, "There He is, the Suffering Servant of Isaiah, who voluntarily bears the judgment of the world's sin"?

The Passover Lamb

Or did John have in mind the Passover Lamb? Israel of old was held in bondage in Egypt. God told Moses that as the final act of judgment against the oppressors, the "angel of death" would go through the land and kill all the firstborn. God told Moses to instruct the people of Israel to each find an unblemished lamb. The people were to kill it and then take the blood of the lamb and spread it using hyssop branches on the doorposts of their homes (Exod. 12:7). And God told Moses, "When I see the blood, I will pass over you, and no plagues will befall you to destroy you when I strike the land of Egypt" (12:13).

John the Baptist sees Jesus of Nazareth coming towards him. It has been suggested that even as John the Baptist saw Jesus, there passed by flocks of lambs, being driven up to Jerusalem from the country districts to serve as sacrifices for the Passover Feast.[10] John sees those lambs, those lambs who recall the lambs by which the Israelites were delivered from slavery and death. And pointing to

Jesus says, "There is the one and only Lamb whose blood can finally deliver." Is that what he means?

The way John the apostle works with the Passover in his Gospel leads in this direction. It is in his Gospel that we learn that Jesus was condemned at noon the day before Passover (John 19:14, 31) at the very time the priests would begin to slay the Passover lamb.[11] It is in John's Gospel that we learn that a sponge full of wine was raised to Jesus's mouth on a hyssop branch (19:29). Hyssop was what the Israelites used to apply the blood of the lamb to their doorposts (Exod. 12:22). It is in John's Gospel that we learn that none of Jesus's bones were broken as He hung on the cross. The Apostle comments on this saying, "For these things came to pass to fulfill the Scripture, 'Not a bone of him shall be broken'" (John 19:36). The verse he quotes refers to the Passover Lamb (Exod. 12:46). Is that the lamb the Baptist had in mind?

The Scapegoat

Or did he have in mind the scapegoat of Yom Kippur, the Day of Atonement? On that highest of Holy Days the high priest was to take two goats. One goat was to be slaughtered as a sin offering. The priest was then to take the other goat and over it confess all the sins of the children of Israel. Then the priest was to lay his hands on the goat, symbolising a transfer of the sin of Israel to the goat. The goat was then sent into the wilderness, carrying away Israel's sin (Lev. 16:20–22).

It is argued that in that moment on the cross when Jesus dies, He is, in fact, all alone; He is all alone in the wilderness of isolation from God, carrying away the world's sin. New Testament scholar Herman Waetjen writes:

> [In that moment, Jesus] became the embodiment of the scapegoat who bears the human infection into the oblivion of nothingness.

Jesus not only uses His suffering to atone for sin and thus to satisfy God's justice, He also inaugurates the abolition of sin without which eradication of sin, the incarnation of God's Kingdom rule could never be actualised.[12]

Even though the scapegoat is a goat and not a lamb, is this what the Baptizer had in mind when he pointed at Jesus?

The Lamb of the Daily Sacrifice

Or did he have in mind the lamb of "the daily sacrifice"? Every morning and every evening an unblemished lamb was offered on the altar in the temple (4:32). The priests were instructed to lay their hands on the lamb, transferring their sin and the sin of the people to the lamb. It was thought that when the lamb then died on the altar, the lamb was suffering the punishment for the people's sin, thus "covering it over" and making possible the restoration of the Divine-human relationship. This act was repeated every day even when the people were starving or at war or under siege.

In addition to the daily sacrifices, a host of others were prescribed. Of particular interest to us is the guilt offering. Although usually a ram, on certain occasions a lamb was used.[13] We even find the expression "the lamb of the guilt offering" (14:12). The offerings of this lamb supposedly took away the guilt of the one making the sacrifice. Interestingly, John the Baptist's father Zachariah was a temple priest, which meant John grew up in the midst of the whole sacrificial system. He knew what the sacrifices were all about. Can we paraphrase his claim the following way? "Every morning and every evening, day after day, year after year, priests like my father offer lamb after lamb. But are we freer of guilt? Are we any more secure in our relationship with the Holy God? Look, there is *the* Lamb who does free us from guilt and restores fellowship with God. Lay your hands on Him and your sin is truly taken away."

Is this not the way the rest of the New Testament sees it? At the cross, the sin of the world is transferred to Jesus. The apostle Paul boldly declares, "God made Him who knew no sin to become sin for us" (2 Cor. 5:21). The Lamb without blemish took upon Himself the sin of the world and shed His blood, thus reconciling the world to God. Is this what John had in mind?

The Lamb God Will Provide

Or did he have in mind the lamb that God provides in the Abraham and Isaac story (Gen. 22)? God had commanded Abraham to sacrifice his only and precious son Isaac on Mount Mariah. Abraham obliges this strange command. Up the mountain he goes, knife in hand, Isaac carrying the wood for the sacrifice. Then they reach the top of the mountain. Isaac asks the question that had been haunting him: "Behold, the fire and the wood, father, but where is the lamb for the burnt offering?" (22:7). Abraham replies, "God will provide *Himself* the lamb, my son" (22:8). An amazing statement, to say the least.

Abraham then prepares the altar. He binds Isaac upon the wood and then, just as he is about to thrust the knife into the body of his son, God stops him and over in the bushes they see the substitute—a ram for the sacrifice. Is this the story in John's mind when he says, "Look! The Lamb of God. God's Lamb"?

According to New Testament scholar Alan Richardson:

> Jewish thought increasingly came to hold that the covenant relationship with God was founded upon Abraham's offering of Isaac. John is asserting that the new relationship of God and humanity in Christ (the new covenant) is based upon the fulfilment of promises contained in Genesis 22:8. That God would provide the lamb, which would make atonement for universal sin. Jesus is the Lamb of

sacrifice promised by God to Abraham, the father of many nations, and thus He is the God-given universal sin bearer.[14]

Is the Baptist saying, "Look! God's own Lamb. No one need offer any more lambs or goats or bulls. No one needs to offer their sons or daughters, for God is offering up Himself as the Lamb"?

So which of these "lambs" did John the Baptist have in mind? Or is it a case of John the Gospel writer's habit of taking a word, which has a variety of meanings, and embracing something of all its meanings? Is it not a case of John seeing Jesus as a composite of all possible meanings of the terms? I think so. Jesus—the Lamb of God—fulfills something of all the "lambs" we've considered.

- He is the conquering lamb, who breaks the back of evil.
- He is the suffering lamb, who exchanges places with sinful humanity.
- He is the Passover lamb, who delivers us from slavery and death.
- He is the scapegoat, who bears the world's infection into the wilderness, inaugurating the eradication of sin, making way for the Kingdom.
- He is the lamb provided to Abraham, whose blood seals the new and everlasting covenant between God and humanity.
- He is the one great final sacrifice, who fulfills all that is foreshadowed in all the sacrifices.[15]

Which is why God's Lamb sheds His blood. He can cry out, "It is finished!" (John 19:30). It is something final, something ultimate and cosmic. Look! Finished!

Because the Lamb Takes Away Sin

The implications for this are many and profound. Let me emphasize two as I conclude.

First, it is safe to be in the presence of Jesus. We can dare to come forward in our sin. For everything that needs to be done about sin has been done! Everything! "There is now no condemnation for those who are in Christ," says the apostle Paul (Rom. 8:1). No condemnation! It's safe.

So Charlotte Elliot could sing:

> Just as I am, without one plea,
> but that Thy blood was shed for me,
> And that Thou bidst me come to Thee,
> O Lamb of God, I come.

> Just as I am, Thou wilt receive,
> wilt welcome, pardon, cleanse, relieve;
> Because Thy promise I believe,
> O Lamb of God, I come.[16]

There is no need to hide anymore. It is safe to be in the presence of Jesus.

Second implication. It is possible to change. The power of the great infection has been overcome. The stronghold of the addiction has been broken. We do not have to be what we have become in the grips of sin. The deeply-rooted patterns of sin can be uprooted. We can change. Finally we can change. *We do not have to yield to sin anymore!* (We do. And we will.) But there is no longer any inherent necessity, for something has been done to sin. And we have been baptized into that something. "Such were some of you," says the apostle Paul to the Corinthians, "but you were washed, but you were sanctified, but you were justified" (1 Cor. 6:11).

This is not perfectionism. This is hope. We can change. Sometimes it feels like an uphill battle. But the good news is *it is no longer our battle.* The Lamb of God takes it up in His battle. We are changed by the power of His victory. Our part? *Yield to His victory.* Be honest, come clean, come as we are and throw ourselves on Jesus.

Got junk? He'll take it! Got junk in "the shack," in the secret places of the heart? He will take it.

"Look! Look! The Lamb of God who takes away the sin of the world!"

2

The One Who Baptizes in and with the Holy Spirit

John 1:19–34

Who is He? Jesus of Nazareth—about whom more books have been written than any other person in history. For whom more songs have been written and sung than any other person in history. Firstborn Son of a humble maiden. Adopted Son of a rugged carpenter. Who is He?

The fact is we will never be done with the question! We will never be done asking it, let alone answering it. Given who He is, given who the New Testament says He is, no one will ever be able to say, "Well, that's it! I have mastered Jesus, time to move on to something more important."

As my friend Dale Bruner puts it, "There are no graduates from the Jesus School." There are only and always undergraduates. Who is Jesus? No question comes with higher stakes. For given *who* He is, given *who* the New Testament says He is, literally *everything* rides on how we answer.

In the previous sermon we turned to John the Baptist for help. We do so again now. Why John? Because all four Gospels—Matthew, Mark, Luke, and John—begin their telling of the story of Jesus with John the Baptist. Why? John is the last in a line of the great prophets: beginning with Elijah, then Elisha, Isaiah, Jeremiah, Ezekiel, Daniel, Hosea, Jonah, Amos, on to Malachi, and finally to John. But whereas the other prophets looked to the day when He would come, John actually gets to announce His arrival! To John was given the great privilege of being the first person to actually introduce Jesus to the world.

So we ask the great Baptist, "Who is Jesus?" And oh, what an answer he gives: "*The LORD*" (John 1:23). "I am a voice crying in the wilderness, 'Make straight the way of the LORD.'" John is quoting from the prophet Isaiah: "A voice is calling, 'Clear the way for the LORD in the wilderness'" (Isa. 40:3).

In that context "the LORD" is the God of Israel. In that context "the LORD" is the Creator of the universe. In that context "the LORD" is Yahweh, the True and Living God. "Make straight the way of the LORD," says the Baptizer. Jesus—LORD? Jesus—the God of Israel? Jesus—the Creator of the universe? Jesus—Yahweh come to earth? Yahweh in human flesh? The name "Jesus" is the English for the Greek name *Iesous*; *Iesous* is the Greek for the Hebrew name "Joshua," or *Y'shua*. *Y'shua* means "Yahweh saves," or "Yahweh-to-the-rescue." Jesus of Nazareth—John the Baptist's cousin—Yahweh-to-the-rescue? "Make straight the way for Yahweh-to-the-rescue!"

No wonder John preached with such passion and sense of urgency! And no wonder John says of Jesus, "He existed before me" (John 1:30). Although Jesus was born six months after John, He existed long before John was conceived in his mother's womb. And no wonder John says, "I am not worthy to untie the strings on His sandals" (1:27). Who is? And no wonder John says of Jesus, "This is the Son of God" (1:34). At the least! At minimum the Creator in our flesh is the Son of God. The only-begotten Son of God the Father, God the Son, who for all eternity exists in the heart of the Father, who in word and deed reveals the Father. *That is who* the great Baptist thinks Jesus is! "Make straight the way of God-to-the-rescue."

And John tells us why the LORD comes, why He comes the way He comes. The Baptist tells us that Jesus comes to do a two-fold work. This two-fold work is expressed in two provocative titles. The first one we considered in the previous sermon: *The Lamb of God who takes away the sin of the world.* The second title is: "*The One who Baptizes in and with the Holy Spirit.*" John the Baptist says: "[The Father] who sent me to baptize in [and with] water said to me, 'He upon whom you see the Spirit descending and remaining upon Him, this is the One who baptizes in [and with] the Holy Spirit'" (John 1:33).

The Son of God—God the Son in our flesh—is the Lamb of God who comes to take away the sin of the world *and* the One who baptizes in and with the Holy Spirit. The two works belong *together.* For it is when the two titles are kept together that the Gospel of Jesus Christ is really good, good news! Yahweh-to-the-rescue takes away the sin of the world (!) and then baptizes human beings in and with the Spirit of God!

John Stott of England put it best in a sermon he preached for the Urbana conference in the early 1970s:

> We must never conceive of "salvation" in purely negative terms, as if it consisted only in rescue from sin, guilt, wrath, and death. We thank God that it is all these things. But it also includes the positive blessing of the Holy Spirit to regenerate, indwell, liberate and transform. What a truncated gospel we preach if we proclaim the

one without the other! And what a glorious gospel we have to share [with the city] when we are true to Scripture![1]

Jesus of Nazareth, the eternally existing Son of the Father, God the Son, comes to take away sin, and to baptize us in and with the Spirit of God! The Lamb of God who takes away sin baptizes! Like His cousin John, Jesus also baptizes. John baptizes Jesus in and with water. Then Jesus baptizes John—and anyone else who welcomes Jesus—in and with the Holy Spirit! The best baptism!

I want to ask two questions about this second of Jesus's two-fold work. Question one: What does "The One who baptizes in and with the Holy Spirit" mean? Question two: When does Jesus baptize us? *What and when.*

What Does It Mean?

What does it mean to be baptized in and with the Holy Spirit, and are there other ways to express what it means? For one thing it means history is reaching a climax point. It means that a great promise is being fulfilled. The great promise to pour out the Spirit of God upon all flesh. In Joel 2:28 we hear the LORD say to His people:

> And it will come about after this
> That I will pour out My Spirit upon all [flesh];
> And your sons and daughters will prophesy,
> Your old men will dream dreams,
> Your young men will see visions.

In Jesus, the great expectation of God Himself pouring Himself on humankind is beginning to be realized! But why the term "baptize"? "This is the One who *baptizes* in and with the Holy Spirit"? What is John the Baptizer getting at? In both pre-biblical and biblical Greek, *baptidzo* simply means "to immerse." Immerse—it was used to describe "sinking in the mud" or "plunging beneath the surface." In its

27

passive form—"be baptized"—it meant "to be overwhelmed" or "to be inundated." Jesus, the Lamb of God who takes away the sin of the world, baptizes *in and with* the Holy Spirit.

You may have noticed that I have been saying both prepositions. The English text uses only one: "in." Why have I been using both "in" and "with"? Because the preposition John uses (*en*) means both "in" and "with." And as is often the case in the New Testament, when a word has multiple meanings, all the meanings are intended. *In and with.* Jesus baptizes *in and with.* "In" calls attention to that into which we are immersed. "With" calls attention to that which overwhelms us when we are immersed.

Here is the Gospel—the Good News! Just as John the Baptist immersed repentant sinners *in* the waters of the Jordan River, so Jesus the Baptist immerses repentant sinners *in* the Spirit of God. And just as those who went into the Jordan River were thus overwhelmed *with* water, so those whom Jesus baptizes in the Spirit are overwhelmed *with* the Spirit. Or, to put it more graphically, Jesus the Baptizer dunks us in and drenches us with the very Life of the Triune God!

Now, being baptized by the Lamb of God ought to manifest itself in our lives in some way, ought it not? I like how Thomas Smail puts it:

> It may be sudden, critical and sensationally transforming;
> it may be slow and quiet and spread over a period [of time].
> The Spirit is symbolized [in Scripture] as dew as well as by wind,
> but even when the dew falls silently, it will make the leaves
> wet and fresh and sweet.[2]

I like that! Wet, fresh, sweet. Being baptized by Jesus the Baptist will manifest itself in different people in different ways. In different personality types in different ways. In different cultural settings in different ways. The one common denominator for all is the experience of *newness*. There is a new quality of life, a freshness, a Divine nearness and intimacy, a different kind of vitality. *Please Jesus, baptize!*

Is there another way to express this good news of the Gospel?

Yes. Theologians use the word "effusion." Effusion: the escape of liquid from its container; free flow. Effusion. (Isn't that a cool word?) Theologians use the word in conjunction with two other words: creation and incarnation. All three—creation, incarnation and effusion—are the works of the Triune God. The work of creation is mostly associated with God the Father, the work of incarnation mostly associated with God the Son and the work of effusion mostly associated with God the Spirit.

Professor of systematic theology J. Rodman Williams makes the point this way:

> We are dealing in effusion with that activity of the Holy Spirit—not possible adequately to describe—wherein He moves in freedom, pervading and filling human reality. This is the coming of God, to occupy and possess, to pervade and permeate, to fill and fulfill. It goes beyond creation and incarnation, not as a kind of third on the same plane, but passing through them, transcending both. Herein God, while remaining transcendent, nonetheless possesses the heights and depths of creaturely existence. It is the filling of human existence with the glory of God.[3]

Dallas Willard, professor of philosophy at the University of Southern California, in his book *The Divine Conspiracy,* uses the word "engulfment."[4] Jesus promises an engulfment in the Spirit of God. He promises to clothe us, dress us, in "power from on high."

Jesus of Nazareth, the Creator incarnate in our flesh, the Lamb of God who redeems us from the grip of sin, *baptizes us,* He immerses us in, soaks us in, engulfs us in, overwhelms us with, lavishes us with, drenches us with the *very life and glory of the Living God*! This wonderful dimension of the Gospel is expressed most clearly for me in the hymn "Spirit of God, Descend upon My Heart," written in 1854. Listen to George Croly's poetic rendering of the good news:

> Spirit of God, descend upon my heart;
>   wean it from earth, through all its pulses move;
> Stoop to my weakness, mighty as Thou art,
>   and make me love Thee as I ought to love.
>
> Teach me to love Thee as Thine angels love,
>   one holy passion filling all my frame;
> The baptism of the heaven-descended Dove,
>   my heart an altar and Thy love the flame.[5]

The author of this hymn knows this effusion, this engulfment. He has been baptized by Jesus in and with the Holy Spirit.

When Does Jesus Baptize a Person?

We come then to the second question I want to ask of John the Baptist's witness to Jesus. *When?* When does the Lamb of God baptize a person in and with the Holy Spirit? When does the effusion take place in our lives? As I see it, there are several possibilities, and each perspective is advocated by serious students of the Scriptures. The three major options are the sacramental, the evangelical and the charismatic.

The Sacramental Perspective

In the sacramental option, it is argued that this effusion happens when we are baptized in and with water. This is the answer often given by those who hold a high view of the efficacy of the ordinances; the view that baptism and the Lord's Supper not only symbolize Gospel realities, they actually affect the realities. Being baptized in and with water, in the name of the Trinity, results in being baptized in and with the Spirit. When a person is sprinkled with or lowered into H$_2$O, Jesus Christ immerses the person in and overwhelms the person with the Spirit of God.

The Evangelical Perspective

The second option is the evangelical perspective. It is argued that this effusion takes place at the time when a person says his or her "yes" to Jesus. It is argued that this effusion is what makes a person a Christian. It is argued that being baptized by Jesus in and with the Spirit initiates one into the Christian life. When we turn around and put our trust in Jesus as Saviour and Lord, He takes away our sin and effuses us with His life.

The Charismatic Perspective

Option three offers the charismatic perspective. It is argued that this effusion takes place sometime after conversion, sometime after becoming a Christian. It is therefore often referred to as the "second blessing." It is argued that one first comes to know the Risen Lord and begins the journey of discipleship. Then after walking with Him for a while, Jesus baptizes the Christian. First we are born again, regenerated and indwelt, and then one day we are anointed, flooded, empowered. It is argued that this is Jesus's own experience. He was conceived by the Spirit, filled with the Spirit from infancy and then at His baptism, empowered for ministry by the Spirit. It is also argued that this "second blessing" pattern is the pattern worked out in the book of Acts, in the story of the emerging church. First, folks are converted by the Spirit; then later on, they are baptized in and with the Spirit.

So, which of these three major options is correct? Sacramental, evangelical, or charismatic?

Discerning Right and Wrong

As I have wrestled with this, I have come to the conclusion that each of the options is wrong, and each of the options is right. And each of the options is wrong and right for the same reason.

You see, each option works from the same assumption, the assumption that Jesus baptizes us only once. We make that assumption because we are ordinarily baptized in and with water only once. But that is not how John the Baptizer sees it. Listen carefully to the way he puts it. "[The One] who sent me to baptize in [and with] water said to me, 'He upon whom you see the Spirit descending and remaining upon Him, this is the One who *baptizes* in [and with] the Holy Spirit'" (John 1:33 [emphasis added]).

Baptizes. Present tense. This is crucial to note. In New Testament Greek the tenses of verbs point to the time of action. But more importantly, they point to the *kind* of action. In Greek, the present tense emphasizes continuous action, and is best rendered "keep on." "Abide in Me and I in you," literally means *"Keep on abiding* in Me and I in you." "All who come to Me and believe in Me will never hunger or thirst," literally means "All who *keep on coming* to Me and *keep on believing* in Me will never hunger or thirst." John the Baptizer is saying of Jesus the Baptizer, "This is the One who *keeps on* baptizing." Continuous action. *Keeps on baptizing.*

That is, John is saying something about the nature and character of Jesus. John is saying that it is the nature of Jesus, the Saviour of the world, to baptize and keep on baptizing, to immerse and keep on immersing, to soak and keep on soaking, to flood and keep on flooding, to fill and keep on filling, to infuse and keep on infusing. This is the One who baptizes not once, not twice, not three times, but again and again and again. *Jesus keeps on infusing His followers with divine life and will keep on doing so until every fibre of our being radiates with the glory of God!* How's that for good news?

You can see then that option one—the sacramental—is right. When we are baptized in and with water, Jesus baptizes us in and with the Holy Spirit. But option one is wrong: this is not the last time He will do it. You can see then that option two—the evangelical—is right. When we surrender to Jesus Christ as Savior and Lord, He baptizes in and with the Spirit of God. But option two is wrong: this is not the last time He will do it. And you can see then that option three—the charismatic—is right. There is a time subsequent to conversion when Jesus baptizes us in and with the Spirit of God. But option three is wrong: the "second blessing" is not the last time Jesus will do it.

The Baptizer's Perspective

In asking John the Baptist, "When does Jesus baptize a person?" we see that Jesus the Baptizer does not baptize just once. Jesus is the One who keeps on baptizing! He is the One who keeps on dunking His people in and drenching His people with His Spirit!

This perspective, I think, is confirmed in what we see happening in the book of Acts. It all begins with Jesus's promise: "You will be baptized [in and] with the Holy Spirit not many days from now" (Acts 1:5).

Then on the Day of Pentecost, the Risen Jesus pours out His Spirit upon the first band of disciples. The text says they were all filled with the Holy Spirit and people thought they were full of sweet wine (Acts 2:4, 13).

But then a few days later, the Living Lord did it again! The text says: "The place where they had gathered together was shaken, and they were filled with the Holy Spirit. . . . And with great power the apostles were giving testimony to the resurrection of the Lord Jesus, and abundant grace was upon them all" (Acts 4:31, 33).

The same band of disciples was dunked and drenched again; they were given another soaking. And as we read the rest of the story we see Jesus doing it again and again.

Embracing Effusion

Why this "keep on" baptizing? I have already suggested the chief reason: *it is the nature of Jesus to keep on giving His life to us!* There is another. We keep on "quenching" and "grieving" the Spirit. "Do not quench the Spirit," the apostle Paul exhorts us (1 Thess. 5:19). "Do not grieve the Holy Spirit of God, by whom you were sealed for the day of redemption," he tells us (Eph. 4:30). Again and again we do and say things that wound and offend the Holy One. We harbour anger, nurture bitterness, gossip about and slander others. We are, therefore, (again and again) in need of a cleansing bath, we are in need of a showering of new grace.

For years Michael Cassidy of South Africa played a leading role in the work of reconciliation throughout the African continent. At one point he became aware of how he was quenching and grieving the Spirit by his critical, judgmental attitude toward another leader of the movement. So he did what the Gospel calls us to do: he reached out to the other leader in love, asking for forgiveness. Later that night, alone in his hotel room, he found himself "strangely alive." Although exhausted from all his work, "strangely alive." Cassidy describes the moment this way: "He (the Spirit) seemed to be bubbling up from within, surrounding from without, ascending from below, descending from above."[6] Jesus had done it again—He had baptized His disciple again!

There is yet another reason for the "keep on." At the beginning of the journey with Jesus Christ none of us is ready to handle the fullness of the Fullness (the effusion). We are, after all, taking about being invaded and permeated by God! By the third Person of the

Trinity! Who can handle being effused by and with God? So the effusion happens in stages, "grace upon grace" as the apostle John puts it (John 1:16). "Being transformed from glory to glory" as Paul puts it (2 Cor. 3:18).

And there is yet one more reason for the "keep on." Not only are we not ready, but many of us are not willing for the effusion to happen. Not willing? Why? Fear. We are afraid that if we were to really open up to Jesus's baptism the effusion might make us look weird. I know that fear! And we are afraid that if we were to really open up to Jesus's baptism we might get swept up into something beyond our control. Am I right? Beyond our control.

Well, the fact is *it is* beyond our control for *He* is beyond our control. We are talking about the Living God, the Creator of all things, coming to occupy and possess. Who can control Him? So, from our fear, we settle for a manageable form of religion and hold the full reality at arm's length. Out of fear we settle for what Michael Green calls a low level of spirituality.[7] Out of fear we try to domesticate the Wind and Fire of God and settle for the predictable, even if it is no longer satisfying.

But the point is we need not fear the effusion—for the simple reason that we were made for this! From the beginning of God's dealing with humanity, God has revealed His great passion to *give His very Self* to the world. From the beginning, God has made it clear that He intends to fill the whole created order with His glory, with all that makes God be God. This effusion does not make us weird—it makes us human! We are finally human. We are finally what we were created to be when filled with and animated by the life of the Triune God.

So, who is He? This Jesus we are seeking to follow in the city? God-to-the-rescue, come as the Lamb to take away the sin of the world. And come to baptize, to baptize again and again in and with the Holy Spirit. And whenever He does, says William Barclay, there enters into our helplessness and fatigue "a surge of new life," and we are freshly empowered "to do the undoable, to face the unfaceable, to bear the unbearable."[8]

Blessed be His name.

3

The Son of Man

Matthew 16:13–28 and Daniel 7:13–14

My wife Sharon and I had the privilege of living in Manila, the Philippines, from 1985 to 1989. During those years God brought into my life a man by the name of Mansour. A big man: six feet three inches tall and 250 pounds. He was born and raised in Iran and, at the time we first met, a Muslim.

Mansour had fled Iran when the Shah was deposed in the revolution led by the Ayatollah Khomeini. Mansour first fled to Hong Kong, and then settled in Manila, where he went to work for a Jewish manufacturing and export business run by an Italian Catholic from New York. Soon after moving to Manila, Mansour met and fell in love with and married the daughter of the Catholic running the Jewish business.

When I became pastor of Union Church in Manila, Mansour's wife had begun worshiping with the Protestant congregation. She was "on fire" for Jesus as she put it. She kept asking Mansour to come and hear the "new preacher in town" who could help him understand why she was "on fire." He finally agreed to do so but for only four weeks, after which she had to agree to leave him alone, to stop bugging him about their Muslim-Christian conflict.

The four Sundays Mansour chose to come happened to be the four Sundays of the Advent-Christmas season. He was, on the one hand, touched by the sights and sounds of the season and, on the other hand, extremely agitated by what I was saying about Jesus. Through his wife, he asked if I would be willing to have lunch with him and let him express his agitation. So we met. The first time was quite tense. The second was more relaxed; I even felt free to encourage him to start reading the Gospel together, beginning with John. The third time we talked about what he had read thus far. Then we met a fourth time in a Mexican restaurant. What a world: a North American Christian of Swedish descent eating Mexican burritos with a Muslim from Iran in Manila.

During lunch he shared that he had finished reading John and was now in Matthew.

"So what do you think?" I asked.

"Never did a man speak the way this Man speaks," he said, referring to Jesus.

I pointed out that one of the temple guards sent to arrest Jesus said the same thing when he returned without Jesus: "Never did a man speak the way this Man speaks" (John 7:46).

And then Mansour began to cry—right there in the Mexican restaurant.

"May I know why you are crying?" I asked.

"Because," he said, "I think I could come to love Jesus."

After a few moments of sacred silence I asked, "Is there more to your tears?"

"Yes," he said, "I am afraid—I am afraid for my family."

"What do you mean?" I asked.

"If I choose to love Jesus, my brothers will think of me as a traitor and may try to kill me." And he just cried and cried. And I with him.

As we were leaving the restaurant he turned to me and said, "Tell me again: why is Jesus worth the risk?"

❦

Matthew 16:13–28, Jesus claims to be "The Son of Man." He asks his disciples, "Who do people say that the Son of Man is?" (16:13). He began to teach them that "the Son of man must go to Jerusalem, suffer and die" (16:21). He says, "There are some of those who are standing here who will not taste death until they see the Son of Man coming in His Kingdom" (16:28).

It is Jesus's use of the title "Son of Man" that puts Him in a class all by Himself. And why He is worth the risk.

First-Century Context

Matthew is careful to tell us that Jesus identifies Himself as the Son of Man in the first century city of Caesarea Philippi. Now, Caesarea Philippi is located some forty kilometers north of the Sea of Galilee at the southern base of the beautiful Mount Hermon.

What we need to know about Caesarea Philippi is that it was famous for its cultural and religious pluralism. The point is that pluralism is not a new phenomenon. Jesus of Nazareth made astounding claims about Himself in the midst of religious pluralism from the very beginning. Jesus is not afraid of pluralism. Jesus can hold His own in the pluralistic marketplace of religions, spiritualities and ideologies.

In its earliest days, Caesarea Philippi was called Balinas in honour of the Canaanite fertility god, Baal. When Greeks invaded the region they changed the name to Paneas in honour of the Greek god of nature, "Pan" meaning "the All." After the Romans moved in, Herod the Great built a huge white marble temple in the city to the glory of the Caesar who had given Herod the city. In that temple, religious services were regularly held in honour of all the Caesars who by that time were beginning to be revered as gods. In Jesus's day, Herod the Great's son Philip ruled the area and changed the name from Caesarea to Caesarea Philippi to distinguish the city form the Caesarea along the Mediterranean Sea and in honour of Caesar Augustus who from his birth was being spoken of as "a son of a god."

It is in that city—in a city much like our city—that Jesus poses the question, revealing His own self-understanding. "Who do people say the Son of Man is?" Who indeed?

It is a fact in history that Jesus of Nazareth's favourite way of speaking of Himself is to use the term "Son of Man." The term occurs in the New Testament eighty times: seventy-seven times on the lips of Jesus referring to Himself and the remaining three times on the lips of others referring to Jesus.

Eighty times! Interesting, because the term most frequently used by others to speak of Jesus is "Christ," which is Greek for "Messiah." It was used so frequently that "Christ" became a substitute name for Jesus. But of all the names, titles or designations available for His use, Jesus of Nazareth chose "The Son of Man," a fact emphasized by all four Gospels.

This, for me, is one of the many data which gives the New Testament the ring of truth. As you likely know, many in our day argue that as the New Testament was being written, the early church put words into Jesus's mouth which He Himself did not say. It is argued that the historical Jesus—the real Jesus—did not actually say what the Gospels report Him to say; we have, instead, the early church's reconstruction of Jesus.

If this is so, how do we explain the New Testament's use of the "Son of Man" title? You see, nowhere else in the available record do we find the early church call their Master the "Son of Man." Except in the case of Stephen the martyr. As he is being stoned to death, he looks up and says, "I see the heavens opened and the Son of Man standing at the right hand of God" (Acts 7:56). The title simply was not being used by any of the congregations of the first century. They were using titles like Messiah, Christ, Lord, Son of God, Logos, Word.

Now, if the early church was putting words into Jesus's mouth, would they not put into His mouth words that they themselves were using? Words like "Messiah" or "Logos"? But nowhere in the record does Jesus use such terms for Himself. He is Messiah. He is Logos, but He does not say so explicitly.

Yet, seventy-seven times He calls Himself "Son of Man." So New Testament scholar Oscar Cullmann writes: "This would be unexplainable if [the Gospel writers] were really the first to attribute the title to Jesus as a self-designation. Actually, they have preserved the memory that only Jesus himself used it this way."[1]

The Grand Scale of the Title

Now, when we line up all the instances in which Jesus uses the self-designation, we discover that, more than any other title, it embraces the totality of His life and ministry. More than any other title! Jesus uses the term "Son of Man" in reference to His earthly work, but also to His future work and to a time before He was conceived in the womb of the Virgin May.

Listen to a litany of some of Jesus's "Son of Man" statements. Notice how this self-designating title is associated with many aspects of His work, thus giving us an expansive view of Jesus's life.

On the day the first disciples encountered Jesus, He said to them: "Truly, truly, I say to you. you will see the heavens opened and the angel of God ascending and descending on the Son of Man" (John 1:51).

To Nicodemus, a leading Rabbi of the day, Jesus says: "No one has ascended into heaven but He who descended from heaven: the Son of Man" (John 3:13).

One day Jesus and His disciples have broken one of the Pharisees' Sabbath rules. In defense of that action Jesus says: "The Sabbath was made for [humanity] and not [humanity] for the Sabbath. So the Son of Man is Lord even of the Sabbath" (Mark 2:27–28).

Mark tells us that the Pharisees were furious.

Another time, four men lowered their paralyzed friend through a hole in the roof so Jesus could heal the fellow (Mark 2:1–11). To their surprise and to the watching authorities' horror, Jesus says, "My child, your sins are forgiven" (2:5). And in defense of that action, Jesus says, "The Son of Man has authority on earth to forgive sins" (2:10).

To the crowds who followed Jesus after He fed the 5,000, He says:

> Do not work for the food which perishes, but for the food which endures to eternal life, which the Son of Man shall give to you. (John 6:27)

> Truly, truly, I say to you, unless you eat the flesh of the Son of Man and drink His blood, you have no life in yourselves. (John 6:53)

> Does this cause you to stumble? What then if you see the Son of Man ascending to where He was before? (John 6:61–62)

As Jesus makes his way south from Caesarea Philippi toward Jerusalem He says, at least three times: "The Son of Man is going to be delivered into the hands of [people]; and they will kill Him, and He will be raised on the third day." (Matt. 17:22–23)

Along the way to the Holy City, the disciples were arguing about who would be the greatest in the Kingdom of God. Jesus called them to Himself and says:

> Whoever wishes to become great among you shall be your servant; and whoever wishes to be first among you shall be slave of all. For even the Son of Man did not come to be served, but to serve, and to give His life a ransom for many. (Mark 10:43–45)

A few days before entering Jerusalem, Jesus has dinner at the home of Zaccheus the tax-collector. During dinner Jesus justifies such scandalous behavior by saying: "The Son of Man has come to seek and to save that which was lost" (Luke 19:10).

During Passover week, just before going to the cross, Jesus was teaching on the end times. Listen to these sayings:

> For just as the lightening comes from the east, and flashes even to the west, so will the coming of the Son of Man be. (Matt. 24:27)

> But immediately after the tribulation of those days the sun will be darkened, and the moon will not give its light, and the stars will fall from the sky, and the powers of the heavens will be shaken. And then the sign of the Son of Man will appear in the sky, and then all the tribes of the earth will mourn, and they will see the Son of Man coming on the clouds of the sky with power and great glory. (Matt. 24:29–30)

> For this reason you also must be ready; for the Son of Man is coming at an hour when you do not think He will. (Matt. 24:44)

Then, the words He speaks at His trial after being asked by the Sanhedrin (the Superior Court of Israel) if He is the Son of the Blessed One. Jesus says: "I am, and you shall see the Son of Man sitting at the right hand of power and coming with the clouds of heaven" (Mark 14:62).

Matthew, Mark and Luke all tell us that after tearing his robes the high priest calls out, "You have heard the blasphemy." And then the court charges Jesus with blasphemy and sends Him to capital punishment.

Why? Why did the religious authorities react so violently to Jesus's use of "Son of Man"? What did the term mean for the people of the first century?

Two Meanings

Human Being

Two basic ideas came to first century minds at the mention of "Son of Man." First, the term was simply a Hebraic or Aramaic way of saying "human being." For example, the psalmist asks the Creator: "What is man that You take thought of him, And the son of man that You care for him?" (Ps. 8:4).

"Man" and "son of man" are in parallel. God even refers to the prophet Ezekiel as the "son of man"—ninety times. It is a way of saying "human being." In using it of Himself, Jesus is affirming His solidarity with us. He is affirming His real, full humanity.

This first basic meaning of the term led some of the earliest Christian theologians to couple Son of Man with Son of God, so that the term affirms the full humanity and full Divinity of Jesus Christ.

For example, Irenaeus of the second century once said (excuse his non-inclusive language): "For your sakes the Son of God became the Son of Man in order that sons of men might become sons of God."[2] The writer of the hymn "Fairest Lord Jesus" seems to follow this line of thought.[3]

But the fact is this line of thought misses the heart of the matter. For, although meaning "human being," the term "Son of Man" meant so much more to the first century minds, so much more.

You see, of the seventy-seven times Jesus uses the title, seventy-six times He uses it with the definitive article "the." He calls Himself "the" Son of Man, not just "a" Son of Man. Which leads us to the second basic idea triggered by the title.

"One Like a Son of Man"

"The Son of Man" reminded first century people of a special figure in the drama of God's salvation of the world. In the seventh chapter of his book, the prophet Daniel tells us of a vision the Living God gave him one night, a vision affecting the course of world history. In the vision, Daniel sees four beasts representing powerful empires in the world; these four beast-empires are brought before the Throne of God, where they are judged. One of the beasts is slain, the rest lose their dominion. Then we are brought into a remarkable scene which Daniel describes:

> I kept looking in the night visions,
>> And behold, with the clouds of heaven
>> One like a Son of Man was coming,
>> And He came up to the Ancient of Days
>> And was presented before Him.
> And to [the one like a Son of Man] was given dominion,
>> Glory and a kingdom,
>> That all the peoples, nations and [those] of every language
>> Might serve Him.
>> His dominion is an everlasting dominion
>> Which will not pass away,
>> And His kingdom is one
>> Which will not be destroyed. (Dan. 7:13–14)

Amazing!

The vision is centred on "One like a Son of Man." *One like.* What Daniel sees cannot be adequately described and so he uses the word "like"—"One like a Son of Man." The prophet sees a towering figure, a "commanding, redeeming, glorious figure" that is *human-like.*[4]

Soon after Daniel's vision was written down and circulated, people stopped using the longer phrase, "One like a Son of Man," and simply used the title "the Son of Man."

Looking at Daniel 7:13–14, carefully note everything Daniel says about this Son of Man. He comes with the *clouds* of heaven (7:13). This is crucial. In the Bible, clouds are often used as signals for the presence of the Divine. Whenever God met Moses in the Tabernacle, a cloud would come and envelop the meeting place (Exod. 16:10; 19:9).

The Son of Man comes with the clouds of heaven. *Of heaven.* He comes riding on a divine chariot, if you will. The imagery is declaring "the superhuman majesty" of the one like a human; the imagery is declaring the figure's supernatural origin and divine likeness.[5]

Notice how this "One like a human" acts when He is presented before the Ancient of Days. The Rabbis observed that this Person does not bow to the Ancient of Days. Why not? Is He a peer of the Ancient of Days? The Rabbis also observed that this Person does not confess His sins. Confessing his sin was the first thing Isaiah felt convicted to do when he caught a glimpse of the glory of God. ("Woe is me, for I am a sinful man.") Why does this "One like a human" not confess sin? Because He is sinless?

Notice that to this figure is given dominion, glory and a Kingdom. Unlike the kingdoms God has given to other humans, this Kingdom cannot be destroyed; this dominion will not pass away.

And note that all peoples, nations and language groups serve this "Son of Man." *All!* He is a universal figure worthy of universal worship impacting the whole of history. All people will ultimately serve and worship Him.

Who Is This Person?

Who is He who comes with Divine investiture?

Who is He who comes before the Ancient of Days without bowing or confessing His sin?

Who is He to whom is given an everlasting Kingdom?

Who is He whom all nations will worship?

As you can imagine, there was, from the time that Daniel had the vision, a great deal of speculation about the identity of this central figure of world history. By the first century, the title "The Son of Man" came to refer to *a heavenly pre-existent Divine Being who would come to earth in the end times to judge the nations and inaugurate the Kingdom of God.*[6] According to German scholar Ethelbert Stauffer: "Son of Man is just about the most pretentious piece of self-description that any man in the ancient Near East could possibly have used."[7]

Surprising Ironies

Sisters and brothers, only one person in history ever dared to use that most pretentious title! Only One.

In light of the meaning of the term we are not surprised that Jesus was always talking about the Kingdom. What was His first sermon? One line: "The time is fulfilled, the Kingdom of God has come near" (Mark 1:15). Of course! For the Son of Man comes to earth to bring the Kingdom of God.

Nor are we surprised that Jesus, this Man of compassion, regularly spoke of judgment. Of course! For the Son of Man comes to judge all the nations of the world (John 5:27).

Nor are we surprised to find Jesus making Himself the issue in that judgment. Again and again, He claimed that what individuals and nations do with Him is the criterion for judgment. That is the point of His famous parable of the sheep and the goats, which begins, "When the Son of Man comes in His glory, He will sit on His glorious throne" and judge the nations (Matt. 25:31). One day the Son of Man will separate the nations, and the basis of separation will simply be what people did with Him as He came to them in the person of the powerless (25:31–46).

Now we can appreciate why the religious authorities reacted so violently to Jesus's words at His trial: "You will see the Son of Man sit at the right hand of power with the clouds of Heaven" (Mark 14:62).

Jesus was claiming to be that towering figure of Daniel's vision! He was claiming to be the pre-existent heavenly peer of God to whom is given the everlasting Kingdom, the sinless One who has the right to judge the nations and exercise authority over all the earth.

He was on trial before the highest religious court. But when He dared to call Himself the Son of Man the tables were turned. The court was on trial before Him! "Blasphemy!" they cried. Indeed, the judges were now not on the side of the Ancient of Days, the Divine Judge of history, but on the side of the beasts being judged!

Surprise! Perhaps one of the greatest ironies in history.

There is yet another twist to the irony. Recall the litany of "Son of Man" statements. Remember that saying, "the Son of Man will be killed"? Actually, Jesus said it at least three times. "The Son of Man *must* suffer and die" (Matt. 16:21). *Must.* It confused the disciples, for nowhere in Daniel's vision does the Son of Man suffer and die. This is why Peter protests, "No, Lord, this shall never happen to You" (16:22). In that one line—*the Son of Man must suffer*—we discover the Gospel. Jesus is the Son of Man, the judge of the world. But He comes into the world first to suffer and, as He says, "not to be served, but to serve and give His life a ransom for many" (Mark 10:45).

In Daniel's vision all people and nations serve Him. Jesus turns everything upside down and instead, serves the world by giving His life as a ransom.

What does that mean? It means that He, the judge, changes places with us. He puts Himself in the place of the defendants. He suffers the punishment for our sins. He ransoms our lives by giving Himself away so that we can live!

The rightful Judge of the whole world takes upon Himself the very judgment He decrees. As the Son of Man, Jesus the Christ has the authority to execute judgment. He comes, and to everyone's surprise, the Son of Man exercises that authority by executing that judgment against Himself!

Implications for the Twenty-first Century

"The Son of Man." What does it mean for us today and tomorrow and Tuesday that Jesus of Nazareth calls Himself by that title? Let me suggest three words around which to gather the practical implications of Jesus's huge claim. The three words are authority, perspective and decision.

Authority

As the Son of Man, Jesus is the final authority over all of life. He says after His resurrection, "All authority in heaven and on earth has been given to Me" (Matt. 28:18). He will not be boxed up in the private religious spheres of life. He will not stay there.

Let all the great church leaders have their say about what it means to be the church in our time; when Jesus, the Son of Man, comes to the podium, His word is the last word. Let all the great sociologists and psychologists have their say about what it means to be human in our time; when Jesus the Son of Man comes to the podium, His word is the last word. Let all the great philosophers and gurus have their say about the meaning of life; when Jesus the Son of Man comes to the podium, His word is the last word. Let all the great political and military leaders of the world have their say about how to achieve justice and peace. Let them each have their turn in the United Nations General Assembly; when Jesus the Son of Man comes to the podium, His word is the last word.

Audacious? Pretentious? Yes—but only if He is wrong about Himself. After Jesus finishes preaching His Sermon on the Mount, the people who heard Him speak—who heard words that cut across the grain of everything they thought abut how to live in the world—said of Jesus, "This man speaks with authority because this man is the Son of Man" (7:28–29).

Perspective

Knowing Jesus is the Son of Man puts our lives in perspective. Rulers and empires will rise and fall but the Kingdom of the Son of Man will last forever. It cannot be destroyed—His resurrection demonstrates that for all time (Eph. 1:19–23).

The new world order inaugurated by Jesus the Son of Man will never end which means that if we live our lives for that Kingdom, we do not live in vain. All that is out of sync with the Kingdom of the Son of Man will one day vanish into thin air. But all that is in sync with His reign is taken up into the Kingdom that endures into eternity.

Thus Desmond Tutu, long before he became a celebrity, long before he was awarded the Nobel Peace prize—could walk into the office of the Minister of Law and Order, into the office of the man who enforced the policy of apartheid and say, "Mr. Minister, we must remind you that you are not God. You are just a man. And one day your name shall merely be a faint scribble on the pages of history, while the name of Jesus Christ, the Lord of the Church, shall live forever."[8]

The future is secure; it all ends at the feet of the Son of Man.

Decision

What are we going to do with Him? He keeps showing up everywhere, in every sphere we live and work. And He keeps asking the question He asked the disciples at Caesarea Philippi: "Who do you say the Son of Man is?" He asks: "What are you going to do with Me today in this sphere of life? Do you believe I am who I say I am? Will you follow Me? Will you trust me? Will you trust Me with your relationships? Will you trust Me with your careers? Will you trust Me with your finances? Will you trust Me with your future?"

Two weeks after that tear-filled lunch in a Mexican restaurant in Manila, Mansour attended a Full-Gospel Business Persons Luncheon. After a simple clear message on the call and cost of discipleship, the speaker asked if anyone was prepared to respond to Jesus. Mansour stood up, all six feet three inches of him, lifted his hands in the air and said, "I love You Jesus. I am Yours. I will risk it all to follow You."

Not long after, I baptized Mansour in an outdoor swimming pool. I do not mind telling you that both he and I were a little nervous; we felt very vulnerable. As we made our way into the water I whispered in Mansour's ear, "If they kill you, I will make sure your family is taken care of." I lowered him in the water, spoke the name of the Triune God over him. He came out of the water and cried out for all to hear, "I am Yours!"

What else can you say to the Son of Man?

4

The Bread of Life

John 6:22–40

Who is He? Jesus. The Man from Galilee. The Carpenter, born and raised in the backwoods, despised village of Nazareth. "Can anything good come from Nazareth?" someone asked. "Come and see," was the reply. Come and see, indeed!

Again, we say of the church I am serving, "We are a community following Jesus with a heart for the city." Jesus—we are following Jesus. A Person—we are a community following a Person.

We are not a community following a program. Nor are we a community following principles to live by. Nor are we a community following a religion, or spirituality or ideology. We are a community following a Person. So who is He? Who is Jesus?

"I Am the Bread of Life," He says (John 6:35, 48). "I"—a Person—"I Am."[1] "I Am the Bread of Life, the Living Bread." One of the most audacious claims anyone has ever made! "Whoever comes to Me shall not hunger, and whoever believes in Me shall never thirst. Eat this bread and you shall live forever" (6:35, 51).

If you have ever spent time in the fourth Gospel, in the Gospel according to John, you know that this is not the first or only time He dares to use those sacred words "I Am." It is the first time He uses them with a predicate, with a noun. But He had already spoken the "I Am" to a woman at a well in Samaria. She wanted to know where she should worship and she liked what she was hearing from Jesus about worship, but said she would wait until Messiah came. To this Jesus said, "I Am, the One who is speaking to you" (4:26). Not just, "I am Messiah for whom you are waiting." But "I Am, the One you are seeking to worship." He would later say to religious authorities who were very upset with Him, "Before Abraham came into existence, I AM" (8:58).

"Bread of Life" is the first "I Am" claim He makes with a noun attached. He will go on to say:

"I Am the *Light of the world*; whoever follows Me will not walk in darkness but have the Light of life" (8:12).

"I Am the *Good Shepherd*: the Good Shepherd lays down His life for the sheep" (10:11).

"I Am the *Resurrection and the Life*: whoever lives and believes in Me shall live even if they die" (11:25).

"I Am the *Way, the Truth, the Life*; no one comes to the Father but by Me" (14:6).

"I Am the *true Vine*; you are the branches. Keep on abiding in Me and I in you, and you will bear much fruit" (15:5).

All audacious in their own way.

"I Am the Bread of Life." Hugely audacious! And a strange way for a man to speak of himself. Bread? Maker of bread, OK. Baker of bread, sure. Giver of bread, yes. But "the bread"? A Person—the bread itself?

We cannot make it without bread; it is absolutely necessary for human existence. We can make it without most of what we have but we cannot make it without bread.

"I Am the Bread of Life. Life does not work without Me. You cannot make it without Me. I am absolutely necessary for human existence. You can make it without most of what you have but you cannot make it without Me." Again, hugely audacious! Jesus is saying, "You need Me *as much as* you need your next meal. Indeed, you need Me *more than* you need your next meal."

I once heard Bruce Metzger of Princeton point out that Jesus does not say, "I Am the Cake of Life." He could say that, for He is delicious in every way, but He does not say that because we can make it without cake. We simply cannot make it without bread. Cake is a luxury, bread a necessity. Had Jesus lived in Asia He might have said, "I Am the Rice of Life." Had He lived in the north latitudes of Canada and Russia and Scandinavia, He might have said, "I Am the Potato of Life." *"I Am not a luxury. I Am absolutely essential for human existence."*

No one ever made such a claim for himself! No one, except the God of Israel. Jesus is saying to our city, "You need Me more than your next meal."

You realize, do you not, that in making this huge claim about Himself Jesus is paying us *a huge compliment.* Jesus is saying that we are the earthly creatures who can only be satisfied by heavenly food. Jesus is saying that we are the creatures whose hunger and thirst can only be met by a Person, by the great "I AM." No earthly bread can meet the deepest longings and cravings of the human person. None of the "stuff" we clamour to own and keep finally satisfies. We are too gloriously constituted for "stuff" to fill us. This is a fact made graphically clear in the wealthy parts of the world, in our part of the world where we have all the "stuff" anyone could ever want and are still hungry. *We are so gloriously constituted that only a Person can meet the longings and craving of our souls.* Our finite hearts can only be satisfied with the infinite "I AM." A huge compliment!

Now, I suppose that Jesus could have made this claim—"I Am the Bread of Life"—anytime, anywhere. He could have said to any hungry, thirsty person anywhere, anytime, "I Am the Bread of Life. Come to Me and eat."

For instance, after preaching His Sermon on the Mount, His exposition of the Kingdom life, He could have said, "In order to live this new way of life, you will need sustenance; I Am the sustenance, I Am the Bread of Life."

But He waited. He waited to make the claim at just the right time, in just the right circumstance. It is another example of His brilliance.

So let us take a closer look at the context. Consider with me five factors which constitute the overall context in which Jesus chooses to say "I Am the Bread of Life." With each factor we uncover rich layers of meaning embedded in Jesus's audacious claim and the brilliance of His timing.

A Miracle

Jesus claims to be the Bread of Life in the context of a miracle—a massive miracle. The apostle John tells us that at one point in His ministry "a great multitude" followed Jesus around the shore of the Sea of Galilee. John seems to underscore the word "great." The multitude had heard and seen the mighty deeds He had been doing, especially His healing of the sick. As the day wore on, the great multitude became hungry. All that Jesus and the disciples had at their disposal was a little lunch brought by a little boy. A little lunch with five little barley loaves and two little fish. John seems to put the emphasis on "little"—great multitude, little loaves of bread, and little fish. "What are these for so many people?" ask the disciples. Very good question! The very question we ask in our time: "What good are our little resources in light of the great number of people in need?"

"Have the people sit down," says Jesus. When they do, Jesus takes the little loaves and little fish, gives thanks to His Father, and begins distributing a lot more bread and fish! The people, says John, "ate as much as they wanted." 5,000 men—plus their wives and children who were not tallied in the count, so upwards of 10,000 people! All eating as much as they wanted. After they had eaten, the disciples picked up twelve baskets of leftovers (John 6:1–14).

Last Monday morning, my wife Sharon and I were at our son's home, about 450 kilometres away. We had driven up there to meet his new son, our new grandson, born the previous Tuesday. Early in the morning, I was sitting in their living room reading my Bible, when our four-year-old grand-daughter Jennifer came to sit in my lap.

"What are you doing, Grandpa?"

"I am reading the Bible. Would you like me to read you a Bible story?" I asked.

"Nope, they are all boring."

"Well, listen to this one," and I told her the story of the feeding of the 5,000.

When I got to the part about Jesus taking five little loaves and two little fish, and how He kept giving more bread and more fish— "more bread, more fish; more bread, more fish; more bread, more fish"—she said, "That's not boring! Are there more stories like that?"

A massive miracle. The only one included by all four Gospel writers. It's more massive than any healing miracle, which is not to minimize His healing deeds—not at all. It is just that in healing, Jesus is taking something that is broken and making it work again. He takes hold of eyes that are not working and makes them see again. Wonderful and impressive. He takes hold of ears that are not working and makes them hear again. Wonderful and impressive. He takes hold of feet that are not working and makes them move again. Wonderful and impressive.

But healing is nothing like what He did in the multiplication of the loaves and fish—where He is taking something and *making more* of it. Very quickly! I cannot get my mind around it. Think of the creativity it takes to speed up the process of baking bread. Think of the creativity it takes to make more fish out of fish!

In that miraculous deed Jesus is demonstrating His ability to provide for human need. He can take little, and out of little, provide much for many. Jesus does not buy into the myth of scarcity that so often rules the world. He knows another world, a world of abundance, which is why in the face of the many He can give thanks for the little. When Jesus comes into the picture, He takes in hand what is there, gives thanks, and provides beyond what we can imagine.

That is the context in which He makes His first "I Am" claim.

A Feast

But there is more to the context: Passover. The apostle John is careful to tell us that "Passover, the feast of the Jews, was at hand" (John 6:4).

Some background. The Passover Feast was, and still is, a time to *remember*—a time to remember God's great acts of salvation when God set His people free from slavery in Egypt. During Passover the Jews remember *with sorrow* the bitter suffering of their ancestors. During Passover the Jews remember *with humility* the sprinkled blood of the lambs, blood which protected them as the angel of death passed through Egypt, blood which caused judgment to "pass over" their homes.

During Passover the Jews remember *with awe* the power of God, how Yahweh the Living God parted the Red Sea so the liberated people could "pass over" to the other side and escape the pursuing armies of the Pharaoh. And during Passover they remember *with gratitude* the gracious gifts of God, how Yahweh miraculously provided manna from heaven and the flesh of quail, so the people could survive in the Sinai desert.

And the Passover Feast was, and still is, a time to *renew hope.* In what sense? Moses—the one who led Israel out of bondage to freedom, the one who prayed for the manna from heaven—this Moses promised that one day God would send another leader, like himself, to speak God's life-giving word. "The LORD your God will raise up for you a prophet like me, from among you . . . you shall listen to him" (Deut. 18:15).

By the first century there was the growing expectation that during some Passover the Prophet-like-Moses would come. And there was the growing expectation that this Prophet-like-Moses would bring with Him the same miraculous deliverance and the same miraculous provision of God. There was a saying in the first century: "As was the first redeemer, so was the final redeemer; as the first redeemer caused the manna to fall from heaven, even so shall the second redeemer cause manna to fall."[2]

That is the context in which Jesus waits to make His "I Am the Bread of Life" claim!

A Challenge

There is a third factor which contributes to the context: a challenge. John tells us that the people were impressed! And John tells us that the people "heard" the nonverbal claim Jesus was making in multiplying bread. "Therefore when the people saw the sign which He had performed, they said, "This is truly the Prophet who is to come into the world" (John 6:14).

This is the Prophet that Moses promised! So impressed are they that they want to seize Jesus and make Him King. Jesus would not have it. He slipped away. He was King alright, but not their kind of king.

The next day the great multitude finds Jesus on the other side of the Sea of Galilee; He had "passed-over." Jesus says to them: "Truly, truly, I say to you, you seek Me, not because you saw signs, but because you ate of the loaves and were filled" (John 6:26).

In John's Gospel, "sign" is a technical word. It refers to a "mighty act" which, though meaningful in itself, nevertheless points beyond itself to a larger reality. The people saw the effect of the sign—5,000 plus people are fed—but failed to see the sign itself. The multiplication of bread points beyond the bread to a gift "that is never exhausted, a satisfaction that never passes."[3] So Jesus exhorts the crowd: "Do not work for the food which perishes, but for the food which endures to eternal life, which the Son of Man shall give to you" (John 6:27).

Now, when Jesus mentions "work" it triggers in the religious mind "good works," works done to earn the blessing and care of God. So the people ask, "What shall we do, that we may do the works of God?" Jesus answers: "This is the work of God, that you believe in Him whom [God] has sent" (John 6:29).

The people are perplexed. What a minute! What did You say? There is only one work you can do to please God—"believe in Me"? Again, hugely audacious. So, the people challenge Jesus. They ask for a sign, for some miracle to validate His claim.

But did He not just give a sign? Is not the feeding of the 5,000 sufficient validation? No, it is not. Why not? And here we are coming to the heart of the matter. The multiplication of the bread is not a sufficient sign because the bread Jesus fed the 5,000 was "bread from *earth*" not "bread from *heaven.*" The bread Jesus miraculously provided by the seashore was not like the bread God provided Israel in the desert. As William Barclay put it, the bread Jesus provided "had begun in earthly loaves and issued in earthly loaves."[4]

Do you hear the challenge posed by the great multitude of people?

They quote from Psalm 78, a psalm that rehearses the Passover events. They say to Jesus, "Our [ancestors] ate the manna in the wilderness; as it is written, 'He gave them bread out of heaven to eat'" (John 6:31).

"He gave them bread out of heaven to eat." To paraphrase the people: "Jesus, we are impressed by what You did yesterday. We really liked the bread You gave us. But even You would have to admit that there is a big difference between what You gave us and what Moses gave our ancestors."

That is the context in which Jesus is making His "I Am" claim.

So Jesus takes up the challenge.

A Sermon

Jesus's response to the challenge brings us to the fourth factor in the context of His "Bread of Life" claim: a sermon form. John is careful to tell us that Jesus makes His claim in the synagogue, that is, Jesus develops His claim within the worship life of Israel. "These things He said in the synagogue" (6:59).

Why is this important for us to know? In the first century, teaching in the synagogue followed a certain form. First, the text for the day was read. Then the preacher for the day would paraphrase the text. The preacher would then comment on each word of the text one by one. Finally, the preacher would conclude by rephrasing his own paraphrase.

In the synagogue the day after feeding the 5,000, the people give Jesus the text. "He gave them bread from heaven to eat," from Psalm

78:24; it is a text that remembers the event in Exodus 16. "He gave them bread from heaven to eat," is the text read in the synagogue service that day.

Now look carefully at how Jesus begins. "Truly, truly, I say to you, it is not Moses who has given you the bread out of heaven, but it is My Father who gives you the true bread out of heaven. For the bread of God is that which comes down out of heaven, and gives life to the world" (John 6:32–33).

Notice what Jesus has done. He clarifies that it was not Moses but God who gave the manna in the desert. Such confusion regularly happens: God does a new work and some human gets the credit. Not Moses but God.

And notice this: God not only gave the bread, but *gives* the bread. Even now. And as sweet as the manna is, it is not the *true* heavenly bread. There is *another* bread that God gives "out of heaven." Manna sustained Israel for only forty years; this *other* bread gives life to the whole world for forever.

The people's appetite is awakened. So is mine! So they say, "Lord, evermore give us this bread" (6:34). Yes Lord! Give *us* this bread too. It is then that Jesus makes His claim.

"I Am the Bread of Life." A Person? Bread?

Jesus then expands on His claim by following the first century form for synagogue sermons.

"He gave them bread out of heaven to eat." Not Moses, but God. Not gave, but gives. Not just any heavenly bread, but the true bread. *"Bread out of heaven to eat."* Then Jesus works with each word one by one.

Bread.

Out of heaven.

To eat.

Bread: "I Am the Bread." This Jesus develops in John 6:35–40.

Out of heaven: "I have come down out of heaven." This Jesus develops in verses 41–51.

To eat: "Eat this bread and you will live forever." This Jesus develops in verses 52–57.

What a context in which to make His claim!

A Story

There is one more layer of meaning to add to the context of Jesus's claim: a story. Jesus makes the claim within a larger story being told and celebrated in the Feast. This is the case with all that Jesus says about anything; He is speaking from within and to a larger story.

A number of important biblical texts were read and reflected on at the Feast. In Exodus 16:4 the text says that God will "rain down" bread from heaven each day. What a promise! Bread from heaven in the desert everyday.

And the text says that the people were to go and gather a day's portion each day except on the day before the Sabbath, when two days' worth would "rain down." The point being that God will provide everyday but only one day at a time and therefore the people will need to go and gather the manna one day at a time.

What does this have to do with Jesus's claim? Jesus says, "I Am the Bread of Life; whoever comes to Me shall *never* hunger, whoever believes in Me shall *never* thirst" (John 6:35).

The word "never" bothered me for the longest time. For there are times, when having come to Jesus one day, I am terribly hungry and thirsty the next. I understand that when I feed on Him I will hunger for more of Him—so there will be hunger in that sense. But I am referring to that sense that I am hungering out of emptiness. "Come to Me, *never* hunger. Believe in Me, *never* thirst." What gives?

The tense of the verbs "come" and "believe"—that is what gives. In the Greek they are in the present tense, which emphasizes continual action: "keep on." Jesus is saying, "keep coming" and "keep believing." Whoever keeps on coming will never hunger. Whoever keeps on believing will never thirst.

The great multitude at Passover understood the "keep coming." The people of Israel had to go and pick up the manna each new day (Exod. 16:22–30). "I Am the Bread of Life. You need to come to Me every day, keep coming." When we find ourselves empty and hungering too much for the bread that perishes, it likely means we have fallen out of the habit of the "keep coming." Keep coming. Keep believing. Every day.

There is another important portion of the Bible read and studied during Passover. It is Genesis 2–3. And Jesus works with that text in His claim.

In Genesis 3 we hear and see the phrase "cast out." Because of the sin of Adam and Eve, the sin of declaring independence from God, which is what eating from the tree of the knowledge of good and evil means—because of that sin, humanity is "cast out" of the Garden of Eden. "So the Lord cast them out" (Gen. 3:24). And the text then says the Lord stationed angelic guards to keep humanity from the Tree of Life. He does not want us to live independently forever. "Cast out." Kept from eating from the Tree of Life.

This text and this theme are in the minds of the worshipers in the synagogue during that Passover. Everyone who heard Jesus speak had the words fresh in mind.

"I Am the Bread of Life." Not just the Bread, but the *Bread of Life*. I wonder if "Tree of Life" was the inspiration for the phrase "Bread of Life"? "I Am the Bread of Life." After making this statement Jesus continues: "All that the Father gives Me will come to Me, and the one who comes to Me I will certainly not cast out" (John 6:37).

Not cast out! Do you hear Jesus? The way to the Tree of Life has been opened. He opened it by dealing with the problem of sin.

"Come to Me; I Am the Tree of Life (?) and I will certainly *not* cast you out!"

Jesus ties into the Genesis part of the story another way, and here we come to the very heart of Jesus's claim. In Genesis 2 God warns Adam and Eve not to eat of the Tree of the knowledge of good and evil. "Do not declare independence from Me—you will not make it. You shall not eat of it lest you die. Eat of it and you will die" (2:17). *Eat of it and you will die.* Then in Genesis 3:6, "She took and ate." And she died. And Adam died. And so did all their children, the whole human race. *Eat of it and die*—the phrase is ringing in the minds of the great multitude that Passover. Eat of it and die. Eat of it and die.

Jesus says, "I Am the Bread of Life. Your ancestors ate the manna in the wilderness, and *they died*" (John 6:48–49). He presses on. Listen! "This is the bread which comes down out of heaven, so that you may *eat of it and not die*" (6:50). Eat of it and not die! Eat of it and not die! *To eat the Bread that is Jesus is to enter into the life we lost at the fall!*

That is the context in which Jesus makes His "I Am the Bread of Life" claim!

So, who is Jesus? Who is this Person we are seeking to follow in the city? "*I Am the Bread of Life!* I Am that without which you cannot live. I Am the final satisfaction of the human soul. Come to Me, every day. Believe in Me, every day. I give you *Myself* as Living Bread."

Which is why the Lord's Supper is the "identifying" feast of the Christian church. When we meet around the Lord's Table to remember His dying for the sin of the world, He comes to us and feeds us. The earthly bread and earthly wine remain earthly bread and earthly wine. But somehow as we eat and drink, Jesus comes and feeds us heavenly bread. He feeds us Himself.

"She took and ate." Took. Ate. Those two verbs do not come together in the rest of the biblical story. We do not find "take" and "eat" together elsewhere—

Until the Bread of Life says, "Take, eat, this is My body given for you." Come. This is the Bread that comes out of heaven and gives life to the world.

"Not cast out."

"Eat and not die."

5

The Light of the World

John 8:12–20

During the process of discerning if the Lord was calling us to the church I now serve, I took some time on two different evenings to walk around the church buildings. The first evening I experienced an overwhelming sense of overwhelming darkness. There were no lights on in the sanctuary and clouds dimmed the light of the surrounding buildings. As I returned to the car I heard a whisper in my soul, "Remember where the light comes from."

After the second evening I left without any such word; I left deeply disturbed. A few days later during a time of worship at Regent College we sang, "Light of the world, You stepped down into darkness, opened my eyes, let me see."[1] He did and I knew we were supposed to join Him, and this congregation, in the heart of the city.

"We are a community following Jesus with a heart for the city." OK, so who is He? Who is Jesus? Who is this Person in our midst?

"Light," He says. "I Am the Light of the world; follow Me and you will not walk in darkness but will have the Light of life" (John 8:12).

Jesus could have and can make that claim to anyone, anywhere, at any time, but He chose to make it in a particular context. When we know more about that context, Jesus's claim—clear enough anywhere, anytime—becomes all the more amazing!

The Feast of the Tabernacles

The apostle John is careful to tell us that Jesus made the claim during Jewish Feast of Tabernacles. He tells us that the Feast of Booths, the Feast of Tabernacles, was at hand (7:2). There are three major feasts which people living within twenty-five kilometres of Jerusalem were obligated to attend: Passover, Pentecost, and Tabernacles. Tabernacles is by far the most popular of the three, for it is the most joyful.

The Feast was, and still is, an eight day celebration held in the fall, early to mid-October. During those eight days, the worshipers live in little huts, or booths or tents, which in Hebrew are called *sukkoth*. This Feast also goes by the name *Sukkoth*.

We have two Jewish families in our neighbourhood; one of the fathers is a professor, the other a surgeon. In the past weeks both built tents in their backyards where the families, as much as possible, ate their meals.

Worshipers live in the tents to recall the days their ancestors lived in tents as they made their way across the Sinai Desert to the Promised Land.

And they live in tents during the Feast as a way to recall that during those days the Living God Himself—Yahweh—graciously chose to live among the people in a tent called the Tabernacle. Hence the name, Feast of Tabernacles.

This most popular Feast is rich in ritual and symbolism. The Feast is constituted around a water ceremony, a light ceremony, and a fundamental theological affirmation celebrated in the festive liturgy.

Briefly, the water ceremony helped recall how God miraculously provided water in the desert. And the water ceremony reaffirmed the great promise that one day God would pour out Living Water, His own Spirit, upon dry and thirsty human souls. It was in the context of the water ceremony "on the great day of the Feast," as John says, that Jesus stood up and cried out: "If anyone is thirsty"—*and who is not?*—"come to Me and drink, and out of your innermost being will flow rivers of living water" (7:37–38).

The fundamental theological affirmation celebrated in the festival liturgy focuses on God's promise to come and dwell among His people forever. In the liturgy we hear again and again God speaking the words "I Am" or "I Am He." This will be the focus of chapter 7 of this book.

The Light Ceremony

Of importance to us now is the light ceremony. The ritual of the Feast is called "The Illumination of the Temple." It took place in the part of the Jerusalem Temple called the Court of the Women, so named because that was as far in as women were allowed to go at that time. This court was a very busy, very noisy place because it was also where the Temple Treasury was located.

On the first night of the Feast, four huge candelabra were set up in the centre of the court. Each candelabrum had four golden bowls on top. They could only be reached by very tall ladders. Floating in the bowls were huge wicks made from the undergarments of the priests. When the sun set, and to the sound of joyful singing, the four candelabra were lit. According to the Jewish Mishnah, all of Jerusalem was aglow in the light![2]

This light ceremony recalled God's gracious guidance of the ancestors in the desert. It was, and still is, very easy to get lost in the Sinai Desert. Even today, with all the advances in transportation and communication, people lose their way. The ancestors had no maps. There were no freeway signs. So God guided them in concrete ways. God set before them a pillar of cloud during the day, and a pillar of fire during the night. Whenever the pillars moved, the people would pack up their belongings and follow. If they did not follow they would be left to walk in the darkness alone.

God's gracious guidance was remembered during the Feast of Tabernacles by reading a number of biblical texts. One text, sung during the Illumination of the Temple was from Psalm 78:

> [We will tell] the generation to come the praises of the LORD . . .
> that they should put their confidence in God
>   and not forget the works of God . . .
> He divided the sea, and caused them to pass through . . .
> Then He led them with the cloud by day,
>   and all the night with a light of fire. (Ps. 78:4, 7, 13–14)

Now, God's gracious guidance points to a basic dimension of God's nature and character: God can guide because God is light. This fact is affirmed throughout the Old Testament, and many of these texts were also read and sung during the Illumination of the Temple. Listen to a few of these texts.

> The LORD is my light and my salvation;
>   Whom shall I fear? (Ps. 27: 1)

> O send out Your light and Your truth, let them lead me. (Ps. 43:3)

> Come, house of Jacob, let us walk in the light of the LORD. (Isa. 2:5)

Arise, shine, for Your light has come,
> And the glory of the LORD has risen upon you. (Isa. 60:1)

No longer will you have the sun for light by day,
> Nor for brightness will the moon give you light;
> But you will have the LORD for an everlasting light. (Isa. 60:19)

For seven nights the people celebrated God as light. On the eighth night the candles were extinguished and the people looked forward to the next year, when light would once again illuminate the Jerusalem night.

Jesus's Brilliant Proclamation

It was on the eighth night that Jesus was walking through the Treasury in the Court of the Woman. "These words He spoke in the Treasury as He taught in the temple" (John 8:20). And in that place, which the night before had been ablaze but was now dark once more, Jesus proclaims, "*I Am the Light. I.* I Am the Light of the world. Whoever follows Me will not walk in darkness but shall have the Light of life."

His claim is brilliant in every sense of the word. Jesus waits until the candlelight goes out. He waits until dark.

It is as though Jesus has said, "You have seen the lights of the candelabra piercing the darkness for seven nights, illuminating all of Jerusalem. I Am the Light that pierces the darkness every night, illuminating the whole world. If you follow Me there will be light not only for seven joyous nights, but for every night and every day. The light of the four candelabra is a glorious light, I know, but in the end it flickers and dies. I Am the Light that never goes out." That is how William Barclay paraphrases Jesus: "I am the Light that never goes out."[3]

It is an enormously staggering claim! Given the necessity of light for human existence, and given the centrality and pervasiveness of light in the religions of the first century—both Jewish and Gentile—Jesus is claiming for Himself cosmic significance.[4]

Indeed His claim is literally "I am the Light of the *kosmos*. Follow Me and you will never walk in darkness."

"Walk in darkness." The phrase makes me shudder. It suggests aloneness. It suggests aimlessness, confusion, fear, even paralysis. It suggests the picture of people grasping for directions, tripping over obstacles they cannot see.

"Follow Me and you will not walk in darkness." Why? Because you "will have the Light of life." You will have the Light that reveals the obstacles in the way of life. You will have the Light that illuminates the path of life. You will have the Light that *is* Life!

"Whoever follows Me." Literally, whoever "keeps on following" Me. The people at the Feast of Tabernacles would have understood the point. Just as the ancestors had to keep their eyes on the pillars of cloud and fire, so we have to keep our eyes on Jesus. Just as the ancestors had to pick up and move when the pillars moved, and stop when the pillars stopped, so we need to be ready to move when He moves and stop when He stops.

"Follow Me. Stay close to Me. Stay right on My heels. I Am the Light of the *kosmos*. Walk with Me and you will never walk in darkness."

Staying Close to the Light

Consider just some of the life-changing implications of Jesus's cosmic claim. How does following Jesus the Light make a difference in our daily lives, one step at a time?

Revealing Who God Is

First, if we stay close to Jesus the Light we will never walk in darkness about God. We will not be in the dark about who God is and what God is like. Jesus the Light leads us out of the vagueness of "God-talk" to know God as God really is. Not all at once of course. In the nature of things that is not possible. It is too much to handle all at once. But step by step, day by day, year by year Jesus reveals the Living God to us.

John tells us that Jesus's Tabernacle claim generates a heated debate. In the claim Jesus says, "If you knew Me, you would know my Father also" (John 8:19). To know Jesus is to know the Father! Later He would say, "Whoever has seen Me has seen the Father" (14:9).

Jesus the Light of the *kosmos* turns out to be the perfect revelation of the true God. He is God-who-is-Light shining into the world in person! The apostle Paul tells the people of Colossae that Jesus is "the visible expression of the invisible God" (Col. 1:15). Paul tells the people of Corinth: "God who said, 'Light shall shine out of darkness' has shone in our hearts to give us the knowledge of the glory of God in the face of Christ" (2 Cor. 4:6). Jesus is God with a face. We know the mystery that is Divinity in the face of Jesus. What is God like? Look at Jesus; God is just like Jesus!

You see, if we begin with the generic word "God," we do not begin with God but with *our own ideas about God*, which are not God.[5] All human ideas about God are less than adequate, some positively misleading. But begin with Jesus and we begin with *God's idea about God*, we begin with God's idea about God's own personal self-revelation. God is just like Jesus. The Father is just like Jesus: just as compassionate as Jesus, just as available and approachable as Jesus, just as merciful and kind as Jesus, just as uncontrollable as Jesus. Stay close to Jesus the Light of the world and we do not walk in darkness about God!

Revealing What It Means to Be Human

A second implication. If we stay close to Jesus the Light we never walk in darkness about humanity. We need not be in the dark about what it means to be human. Jesus is not only the perfect revelation of who God is—He also turns out to be the perfect revelation of who we are, of who we were created to be. Jesus is the one untarnished, untwisted, authentically whole human being.

And what stands out about Him as we watch Him live the truly human humane life? He lives by faith. He trusts His Father. He loves His Father, delights in His Father, obeys His Father. So much so that He can say, "My food is to do the will of Him who sent Me" (John 4:34).

And Jesus loves others. He loves others with His whole being. He finds fulfillment as a human in giving His life away in servant love (Phil. 2:5–11). Jesus is what we were created and are being redeemed to be: persons who believe and love. Jesus is what it means to be human. Believing and loving.

Which is why we both run to Him and from Him. We run to Him because we see in Him what our hearts long to be. When we find Him we feel we have come home. And we have!

We run from Him because in His light we see—painfully at times—how far short we have fallen from who we were meant to be. We do not believe as we ought and we do not love as we ought. We feel ashamed. That is not His intent—to shame us. It is just that the light of His presence exposes the shadows and corners where we hide. Since nothing can be hidden in His presence, we flee from Him—even as we want to run to Him.

Yet we do not flee for long. For one thing, He is inescapable. But for another, we crave what we see in Him.

So, just as we do not begin the search to know God with the word "God," so we do not begin the search to know humanity with the word "humanity." We do not begin with ourselves. We begin with Jesus, the one true human. We begin with Him who is all we were created to be.

In 1928, a gathering of the International Missionary Conference was held in Jerusalem, on the Mount of Olives. It lasted fifteen days. Those in attendance included Archbishop William Temple and missionaries like Robert Spear and John R. Mott. I wish I could have been there. At the end of the conference they issued a profound simple statement. "Our message," they said, "is Jesus Christ. He is the revelation of who God is and of who we, through Him, may become." In Jesus we see who God is and who we, by His grace, are being redeemed to be.

So E. Stanley Jones could say, "There is nothing higher for man or God than to be Christ-like."[6] There is no greater compliment than "You are just like Jesus"—for a human being or for God! "You are just like Jesus."

Stay close to Jesus the Light and we never walk in darkness about Divinity or humanity.

Exposing the Truth about the Human Condition

The light Jesus sheds on Divinity and humanity leads us to a third implication. If we stay close to Him, we never walk in darkness about the nature of the human predicament. We need not be in the dark about what keeps us from being like Jesus, from being fully human. The Light of the *kosmos* reveals the real truth about our predicament.

One of the most effective Secretary Generals of the United Nations was U Thant of Burma-Myanmar. Speaking before an audience of some 2,000 world leaders who had met to discuss the condition for world peace, U Thant expressed his bewilderment. He asked:

What element is lacking so that with all our skill and all our knowledge we still feel ourselves in the dark valley of discord and enmity? What is it that inhibits us from going forward together to enjoy the fruits of human endeavour and to reap the harvest of human experience? Why is it, that for all our profound ideals, our hopes, and our skills, peace on earth is still a distant objective seen only dimly through the storm and turmoil of our present difficulties?[7]

What is wrong with the world? In the presence of Jesus the Light we realize that our problem is not greed, though greed is a symptom of the problem. In the presence of Jesus the Light, we realize that our problem is not racism, though racism too is a symptom of the problem. In the presence of Jesus the Light we realize our problem is not sexism, though sexism is a symptom. Our problem is not nationalism or militarism, though both are symptoms. Our problem is not disease, though it, too, is a symptom. Our problem is not addiction or abuse though they, too, are symptoms.

In the presence of Jesus the Light we see that our problem is much deeper, much more sinister.

Jesus speaks of our predicament in a way no one else ever has. Jesus shows us that we are caught in a complex web from which we cannot free ourselves. "Something" has got a hold on us, and we cannot break its grip. That "something" is a combination of the forces of sin, evil and death. The problem, according to the Light of the world, is that we come in bondage to sin, we're held hostage by the power of evil, and we live in the grip of death. What makes it so bad is that the bondage blinds us so that we do not see the true nature of our condition.

Because He loves us, He exposes the terrible truth. It was during the Feast of Tabernacles that He said, "You will know the truth, and the truth will make you free" (John 8:32). He tells us that none of us can do anything about the real problem. We are powerless against sin, evil and death. We stand in need of a Redeemer. We stand in need of someone stronger than sin, evil and death. We stand in need of Him.

Stay close to Jesus and we no longer walk in the darkness about what ails us. Nor are we in the dark about what finally heals us. I can hardly wait until Christmas when we again hear the angel tell Joseph to call Mary's child "Jesus" for He, Himself, will save His people from their sins (Matt. 1:21). And when we again hear the angel tell the shepherds, "For unto you is born this day a Saviour who is Christ the Lord" (Luke 2:11).

Illuminating God's Plans

This brings us to a fourth implication of Jesus's great claim. Stay close to the Light of the world and we do not walk in darkness about the will of God. He leads us out of the darkness, into the light of God's good purposes. He opens up God's great plans for us and opens up the way to walk into those plans.

Again, not all at once. As God led the Israelites across the desert one step at a time, one day at a time, one week at a time, one year at a time, so Jesus the Light leads us one step at a time, one day at a time. He does not lay out for us a master blueprint for our lives. He does tell us where it all ends—being conformed to His image in a transformed creation. He does not lay out a detailed image of how He will take us there.

When I was ordained to the preaching ministry I never imagined going to Manila. I never imagined coming to Canada. When I accepted the appointment at Regent College ten years ago I figured I would be there well into the retirement years. Little did I know that at age sixty-one I would be one of the pastors of an historic church in the core of a world-class city. He does not give us the master plan for our lives. He gives us Himself—as Bread, as Water, as Light. And step by step unfolds the Father's will for us.

This is how it was for Jesus in His earthly life. Lesslie Newbigin, who lived most of his life in India, writes:

> Jesus had no program of his own. He planned no career for himself. He sought no "identity" for himself, no "image." He simply responded in loving obedience to the will of his Father as it was presented to him in all the accidents, contingencies and interruptions of daily life . . . in the Roman Empire. . . . Only thus did Jesus "abide" in the love of His Father. So the disciples will "abide" in the love of the Father by following [Jesus] along exactly the same road. Disciples will not be concerned to create a career for themselves. They will leave that to the wise husbandry of the Gardener who alone knows what pruning, what watering and feeding, what sunshine, what rain, what warmth or cold is needed to produce the fruit he desires. The disciples will "learn obedience" by following Jesus in the same kind of moment-by-moment obedience to the will of the Father as it is disclosed in the contingent happenings of daily life in the place and time where God has placed them.[8]

This gives me much comfort as I enter into ministry in the city with you. I have many dreams, as you know, about what First Baptist is to be and do at this time in history. And so do you. But the only dreams that finally matter are His.

Clearly, following Him into His dream will mean change. How could it be otherwise? But all change, however good, is experienced as loss. And with loss, the temptation is to run to the past, like the Israelites in the desert. The uncertainty inherent in the journey to the Promised Land was too much to bear. They wanted Moses to take them back to the "good old days" in Egypt. But God in His mercy would not let them go back. He had better plans for them and called them to follow Him into His yet-to-be-unfolded goodness.

Jesus the Light knows where He is taking His church. He knows where He is going and He will not leave us to walk in the darkness about His will.

Replacing Our Darkness with His Light

We come now to the fifth implication of Jesus's cosmic claim. If we stay close to Him, if we dare to take the risks and follow Him into deeper intimacy with Him, we will experience more and more inner cleansing, inner healing. As Light, He moves into the secret places of our lives—into the "shacks" of our hearts, into our thought life, into our emotional fantasies—to expose any and all darkness and burn it away. Like radiation therapy, the intensity of the Light kills the cancer cells of the deepest darkness in our lives. And we begin to experience more and more of what we might call "inner radiance."

As the sun shines on plants causing them to grow and bear fruit, so the Son of God shines in us causing us to mature and bear the fruit of His perfect humanity. Our bodies may decay but not our souls. There will be an "inner radiance."

It all depends on where we fix our attention: on the darkness around us and in us, or on the Light of the world around us and in us.

> Joyful, joyful, we adore thee
>   God of glory, Lord of Love;
> Hearts unfold like flowers before Thee,
>   Opening to the sun above.
> Melt the clouds of sin and sadness,
>   Drive the dark of doubt away.
> Giver of immortal gladness,
>   Fill us with the light of day.[9]

So, who is He? Jesus, whom we are seeking to follow in the city? "Light," He says. "I Am the Light of this whole world. Whoever follows Me shall not walk in darkness but will have the Light of life."

6

The Stronger Man

Mark 3:20–30

Who is Jesus? As we are discovering, the more important form of
the question is, "Who does Jesus think He is?" "The Strong Man,"
He answers. Or more accurately, "The Stronger Man." The person
in our midst is the Stronger Man, who comes to invade a strong
man's house. And once He invades the house, He binds the strong
man, takes away the strong man's armour, and begins to plunder the
strong man's house.

What is Jesus talking about? According to Mark, one of the four
Gospel writers, no sooner had Jesus come on the scene when weird
things begin to happen. Oh, really good things begin to happen!
Like people being healed of all kinds of diseases, like lepers being
cleansed and the blind receiving sight. But weird things begin taking place—at least on modern and postmodern terms. Jesus would
simply show up and demonic powers would cry out, "I know who
You are! The Holy One of God" (Mark 1:24).

Jesus would simply walk into a space—a synagogue, for instance—and before saying a word or doing anything, "unclean spirits" as Mark calls them, would cry out, "What do we have to do with You, Jesus of Nazareth? Have You come to destroy us?" (1:24). On nearly every page of the first half of the Gospel of Mark we find Jesus encountering what Mark further calls unclean spirits: agents of the evil-one himself.

I have to confess that I would just as soon skip over texts like the one before us. But I cannot. For one thing, there are simply too many of them! To skip over them would be to skip over too much of the Gospels' portrait of Jesus. For another, it turns out that Jesus's encounter with evil in the form of unclean spirits is fundamental to the Gospels' portrait of Jesus.

The Gospel writers, especially Mark, would tell us that we will never understand who Jesus is apart from His love for and trust in the One He calls Father. So we will never understand who Jesus is apart from His engagement with and power over the one He calls Satan.

So, what are we—twenty-first-century people living in sophisticated, world-class cities—to make of Mark 3 and other texts like it?

Making Sense of the Demonic Realm

First century readers of Mark would not be surprised that Jesus would have these weird experiences. The whole ancient world believed in demons and devils. They would have no trouble singing with Martin Luther, "though this world with devils filled should threaten to undo us."[1]

The great German historian Adolf Harnack, speaking of the first century understanding of reality tells that "the whole world and the circum-ambient atmosphere were filled with devils; not merely idolatry, but every phase and form of life was ruled by them. They sat on thrones, they hovered around candles. The earth was literally a hell."[2]

First century persons lived in fear of the demonic. So to a first century reader of Mark, the weird happenings are not weird. Different than anything they had witnessed before—which we shall see—but not weird.

But how are we in this "secularized" age—though one has to wonder how secular we are given the amount of money now spent on Halloween—how are we to process the stories of Jesus and the demonic?

It seems to me that we have three options.

The first option is to say that such events did not really occur. To say that Mark has simply drawn his portrait of Jesus in terms of how people of that day feared the demonic, and since Mark knew that Jesus frees people from fear, Mark (and the other writers of the New Testament) created these stories hoping thereby to comfort troubled souls.

The second option is to say that these stories of demons and demon activity are but primitive ways of describing broken reality. We in our day, this option suggests, now know better. We now know that the phenomena first century people attributed to demons can now be explained by "natural" causes, by physical, chemical, psychological, and neurological factors. This option would argue that Jesus, wishing to meet people on their own terms, accommodated Himself to their understanding of reality. If people believed that some of their hurts and disorders were caused by demonic spirits, then Jesus worked on the level of that belief. Instead of trying to change their belief system, their basic worldview, Jesus simply entered it. But, this option argues, Jesus Himself did not hold such an understanding of life.

The third option is to take the New Testament stories on face value, that is, to say that Mark (and the other Gospel writers) is describing what actually happened. This third option says that although they cannot be described with scientific precision, there really are such entities as unclean spirits. Such spiritual beings are, in the words of New Testament scholar James Dunn, "particular manifestations of the evil in the world that is hostile to God."[3] This option says there really is in the universe a personal spiritual force hostile to God. And just as the Living God has spiritual beings called angels to do His bidding, so the enemy of God—Satan—has spiritual beings to do his bidding. This third option says that Jesus never "accommodated Himself to anything He regarded as superstition or error."[4] Jesus never hesitated to correct what He regarded as an erroneous view of life. This third option says that Jesus acknowledges that evil spirits exist and that they can and do gain a measure of control in the world and cause all kinds of disorder and destruction. This third option says that Jesus comes for the express purpose of destroying the works of the devil (1 John 3:8).

I submit to you that the third option is the one that finally makes sense of the data. I realize that in taking this interpretation of the Gospel stories one can be dismissed as an extreme literalist or even as foolish. I realize that in taking this interpretation one faces a host of really difficult questions like: how does the idea of the demonic relate to the insights of modern physics and psychology? Do demons still operate in the world and get a hold on people? If they do, how can we discern when that is the case? And if it is the case, what are we to do?

C. S. Lewis helps us. In his great work, *Mere Christianity*, Lewis makes the observation that the devil "always sends errors into the world in pairs—pairs of opposites. And he always encourages us to spend a lot of time thinking which is worse. You see why, of course?

He relies on your extra dislike of the one error to draw you gradually into the opposite one."[5]

Regarding the demonic, the two opposite errors are: on the one hand, becoming so interested in the demonic that we think we see a demon under every bush; and on the other hand, ignoring and discounting this dimension of reality altogether. Canadian psychologist John White put it so well in his book *The Fight*:

> The devil welcomes a Hume or a Faust with equal zest. He is equally delighted by an atheist, a liberal theologian or a witch. And it may be added he feels as happy with a Christian mind pre-occupied with demons all day long as he is with a Christian mind who never gives them a thought.[6]

Applying a Biblical Worldview

Texts like Mark 3 force upon us the whole matter of worldview; they make us evaluate again our vision of reality. James Sire, for years the editor of InterVarsity Press, defines worldview as "a set of presuppositions (or assumptions) which we hold (consciously or subconsciously) about the make-up of the world."[7] Whether we can articulate the presupposition or assumption is not the point; the point is every individual and every culture has these assumptions.

N. T. Wright calls worldviews "the lenses" through which a people, a society looks at their world, "the grid upon which are plotted the multiple experiences of life."[8]

The worldview that dominates most cities of the world is what we might call a secular worldview. The secular worldview is essentially two-dimensional consisting of (1) the human self and (2) the physical universe.

It is thought that everything can be understood or explained by these two dimensions: the human self and the physical universe.

Everything that happens has its cause in one or both of these two dimensions.

The biblical worldview, however, is four dimensional. There are the two easily recognised dimensions of (1) the human self and (2) the physical universe, but there are also (3) the Living God, and (4) unseen, created "spiritual" beings and powers.

Everything has to be understood, explained, accounted for multidimensionally. The biblical authors tell us that we are not being realistic about life unless and until we factor in all four dimensions of reality. The biblical authors would tell us "secularized" people—that for all our hard-nosed "realism"—we are not being realistic enough! When trying to understand what is happening in our lives or in our cities or in our world, we have to take into account the human self, the physical universe, the Living God, and the unseen, created, "spiritual" beings and powers—all four dimensions.

Biblical realism: it's four-dimensional. If we want to understand life in the universe, on the planet, in the city, we have to factor in the stories of Jesus's encounter with evil spirits.

Again C. S. Lewis helps us, this time in his book *Screwtape Letters*. He writes:

> It seems to me this four-dimensional worldview . . . helps to explain a good many facts. It agrees with the plain sense of Scripture, the tradition of Christendom, and the beliefs of most people at most time. And it conflicts with nothing that any of the sciences has shown to be true."[9]

What are we to make of texts like Mark 3? We are to take them at face value. We are to let them challenge and shape our worldview so that we live more realistically.

Understanding Jesus's Parable

Now, the important question is, what does Jesus make of all that was happening when He simply showed up? This brings us to His first parable recorded in Mark 3.

Mark tells us that Jesus's "own"—apparently referring to His close relatives—were quite concerned about Him. Having heard reports of what was happening, especially about Jesus's encounter with unclean spirits, some concluded that He was going mad. "He has lost His senses," they say (3:21). The professional theologians, the scribes and the Pharisees, were also concerned. "He is possessed by Beelzebub," they say. "He casts out demons by the ruler of the demons" (3:22).

The scribes had no trouble accepting the factuality of Jesus's exorcism; they questioned the source of Jesus's power. They concluded that Jesus was in cahoots with Satan himself! Jesus points out the logical inconsistency of their analysis:

> How can Satan cast out Satan? If a Kingdom is divided against itself, that Kingdom cannot stand. If a house is divided against itself, that house will not be able to stand. If Satan has risen up against himself and is divided, he cannot stand, but he is finished! (Mark 3:23–26)

Jesus then warns the scribes to be very careful how they analyze Jesus's deeds. To attribute the work of Jesus to the demonic can lead to the unpardonable sin.

Then Jesus gives His own analysis of what is going on in His first parable: "No one can enter the strong man's house and plunder his property unless he first binds the strong man, and then he will plunder his house" (Mark 3:27).

Luke records a fuller telling of the parable: "When a strong man, fully armed, guards his own house, his possession are undisturbed;

but then someone stronger than he attacks him and overpowers him, he takes away from him all his armor on which he had relied, and distribute his plunder" (Luke 11:21–22).

In this parable Jesus is revealing His worldview. He is revealing His own understanding of *the fallen human condition* and is revealing His own understanding of *His role in the world*.

A House under Siege

According to Jesus, the world is a house under siege, occupied by a strong enemy. Beelzebub, one of the names Scripture gives to Satan, means "lord of the house."

In His parable Jesus is offering what the rest of Scripture teaches. At some point in time, before God created the world, one of the angelic beings whom God made rebelled. Why? All we are told is that this being, created to serve God and God's purposes, did not want to accept God's lordship over his own existence. So he declared independence and began an angelic revolution. That decision brought evil into existence. God created no evil; nothing God made was originally evil. This being—Satan, devil, accuser—became evil as a result of his decision to be independent of God.

Since that time, this personal source of evil has been committed to thwarting God's purposes in the world. He has worked so hard and gained such influence that the apostle John can say, "the whole world lies in the power of the evil one" (1 John 5:19). Behind the movements of human history, behind the powerful human structures that oppress people, lies the operation of what the apostle Paul calls "principalities and powers," or "powers and dominions, rulers and authorities," a whole host of demonic agents carrying out Satan's designs (Eph. 6:12).

According to Jesus's parable, these demonic forces have infiltrated our existence and in some way hold humanity hostage.

More than that, God's enemy seeks to destroy humanity. Not because he hates us but because he hates God; he wants to destroy God. But since he cannot get at God, he goes after what God has made, especially human beings, creatures made in God's image. Since he cannot get at God—for he is not God's equal—he goes after what is closest to God's heart. Humans.

Like the Mafia. When the Mafia cannot gain control over a businessman, they go after the man's family and they kidnap his children.

The world is under siege by a strong man.

Liberating the Hostages

In His first parable Jesus reveals what He has come to do. He has come to plunder the strong man's house! He has come to set the hostages free!

In his *Ceremony of Carols*, Benjamin Britten sets the following poem to music:

> This little Babe so few days old,
> is come to rifle Satan's fold;
> All hell doth at his presence quake
> though he himself for cold do shake;
> for in this week unarmed wise
> the gates of hell he will surprise.[10]

So, for example, in the ninth chapter of his Gospel, Mark tells us of a boy with symptoms akin to epilepsy being brought to Jesus. Jesus sees through those symptoms to the presence of evil and without the magical spells and elaborate incantations of other exorcists, Jesus simply speaks a word: "You deaf and dumb spirit, I command you, come out of him and do not enter him again" (Mark 9:25).

In the fifth chapter of his Gospel, Mark tells us about a man with a violent, uncontrollable personality. Mark says of the man: "No one was able to bind him any more, even with a chain" for he would tear the chains apart (5:4). Jesus sees through the abnormal behaviour to the presence of not one but a legion of spirits. And again, without any fanfare, He simply spoke, "Come out of the man, you unclean spirit" (5:8).

Now we must be careful here. Jesus does not attribute all sickness, personality disorders or violence to the demonic. Most illness and most disorder is due to the brokenness of creation and to the sin of humanity. Jesus comes into all the wreckage to make us whole again. Sometimes we need forgiveness. Sometimes we need physical healing. Sometimes we need psychological healing. And sometimes we need to be delivered from the work of Jesus's enemy.

Binding the Strong Man

Jesus is the Stronger Man who comes to plunder the strong man's house. He comes to set the captives free. He does it by binding the strong man. Not by destroying him—not yet—but by binding him.

This binding Jesus begins to do in the wilderness when Satan comes to test Him. Three times the enemy tries to deflect Jesus from His mission. Three times Jesus stands. Jesus wins all three rounds and emerges from the wilderness with His Gospel: "The time is fulfilled, the Kingdom of God has come near" (1:15).

But the real "binding" takes place at the cross. As Jesus is being arrested He says to Judas and the soldiers, "When I was with you day after day in the Temple, you did not lay hands on Me. But this hour and the power of darkness are yours" (Luke 22:53).

Jesus is now moving into the final confrontation. The soldiers take Him away and He does not resist. *This* is being stronger than the strong man? During the mockery of a trial He does not defend Himself. *This* is being the Stronger Man? While being beaten and spat on He does not retaliate. *This* is being the Stronger Man? He is forced to carry His own cross up the hill to Golgotha. *This* is the way to bind evil?

The forces of evil, I am sure, were delighted with Jesus's behaviour. The evil one's henchmen had to be rejoicing. I can imagine them saying, "So, Jesus of Nazareth, You have come to destroy us, have You? You won in the desert but now You will be defeated." Finally Satan was going to get at God, as God Himself is in the person of Jesus.

And then Jesus dies and more strange things begin to happen. The curtain in the Temple is torn in two. The earth begins to shake. The rocks split and graves were opened. Graves were opened? As Jesus lets evil take Him down, graves were opened? Yes, because in the moment Jesus dies, death lost its grip. Jesus's death is the death of death! As a mentor of mine once said, "When death stung Jesus, it stung itself to death." Death had to let its captives go.

This means Jesus had just robbed the strong man of his greatest weapon: the fear of death. The strong man could no longer hold the hostages with the threat of death. Death is no longer the boogeyman it once was. Jesus has defanged death. And as the writer of the book of Hebrews puts it: "Through death [Jesus] might render powerless him who had the power of death, that is, the devil, and might deliver those who through fear of death were subject to slavery all their lives" (Heb. 2:14–15).

Just before Jesus dies the powers of evil were rejoicing! "Finally, we got Him, and with Him all He has created." But in the moment He dies the rejoicing stopped. Evil was hit with the realization that Jesus had just won the victory!

This is what Mel Gibson tried to show in his movie *The Passion of the Christ*. Remember that snake figure sneaking around at different times in Jesus's life? He is moving in the background as Jesus stands before Caiaphas and Annas, the high priests. He is moving in the background as Jesus stands before Pilate. And he is slithering in the background as Jesus is dying on the cross.

But remember what happens in the moment Jesus dies? The snake, the evil one, screams out in desperation, and whirls down, down, down. Why? In the moment Jesus died He overcame the evil one. The Stronger Man, taking what appeared to be a weak way, had bound the strong man!

And on Easter morning the Stronger Man came out of the tomb and continues to plunder the strong man's house. The Lamb of God who takes away the sin of the world turns out to be the Lion who takes down the ruler of evil.

Because Jesus Is the Stronger Man

So what are the implications for us at this time in history in this place?

First, the personal implication. We need not fear the evil one in his desire to destroy. We can now say to him, "Jesus has bound you. You have no authority in my life. Be gone." In those times when we sense we are being hassled, tormented or attacked by evil, we can take our stand in Jesus and in His name say, "You leave me and my family alone." I had to do that a number of times this past week as I struggled to write this sermon. A number of times I just wanted to give up and preach an easier text. A number of times I put my pencil down and said, "You leave me alone; I belong to Jesus. I am going to tell the truth. You may be strong but Someone stronger has bound you. Back off!"

And second, the social implication. Jesus has given His disciples His authority over the demonic. Matthew, Mark and Luke all emphasise the fact (Matt. 10:1; Mark 6:7; Luke 9:1). So when the seventy disciples returned from the short-term mission project on which Jesus had sent them, they tell Jesus with joy, "Lord, even demons are subject to us in Your name." *In Your Name.* There is authority and power in Jesus's name!

So we read in the books of Acts stories of how the church was used to set captives free. In the city of Philippi, for example, the apostle Paul and Luke the physician are being hassled by a certain slave girl. She had a "spirit of divination," as Luke calls it, and was bringing her masters quite a fortune by storytelling. She kept following Paul and Luke crying out, "These men are bond-servants of the Most High God, who are proclaiming the way of salvation" (Acts 16:17). She kept it up for days. Finally Paul had enough. He turns around and says—not to the girl but to the spirit, "I command you in the name of Jesus that you come out of her" (16:18). And it did. The girl was free and the Gospel went forth in power.

The church never need cower in the face of evil. Indeed, the church can now dare to move into Satan's strongholds, and in Jesus's name announce the release of hostages. "I will build My church," says Jesus, "and the gates of hell shall not prevail against it" (Matt. 16:18). Most people have taken this to mean that as Jesus builds His church in the world, hell will try to destroy it but will not succeed. This is true. The powers of hell will try and will not succeed. But what Jesus is really saying is that He will build His church and *the church will move into hell's strongholds* and hell will not prevail against the church!

This is why, when the Gospel is announced in a city, the city begins to change. Not only because individuals begin to change, but because the powers of darkness and deceit, the forces of oppression and exploitation are *moved*.

One of my favourite contemporary Christian songs is the one by Newsboys entitled "He Reigns": "It's all God's children singing, 'Glory, glory, hallelujah, He reigns, He reigns.'" Then this line: "And all the powers of darkness tremble at what they've just heard."[11]

That happens every time we worship in the name of Jesus. The powers of darkness tremble for they once again realize that Jesus, the Stronger Man, has bound them.

You spirits behind pornography: as strong as you are, Jesus is stronger, and He binds you. You must let the captives go free.

You spirits behind human trafficking: Jesus is stronger than you and He binds you. You must let the captives go free.

You spirits behind drug abuse: as strong as you are, Jesus is stronger, and He binds you. You must let the captives go free.

You spirits behind gang warfare in this city: Jesus is stronger, and He binds you. You must let the captives go free.

You spirits causing confusion in this city: Jesus is stronger, and He binds you. You must let the captives go free.

> And though this world, with devils filled,
>   should threaten to undo us,
> We will not fear, for God hath willed
>   His truth to triumph through us;
> The prince of darkness grim,
>   we tremble not for him;
> His rage we can endure,
>   for lo, his doom is sure;
> One little word shall fell him.[12]

This little word is the name "Jesus."

7

"I Am He"

John 8:21–58

The question began to haunt me while attending university studying physics and theoretical mathematics. I had freshly fallen in love with Jesus. I say "freshly fallen in love" because there is a sense in which, as far back as I can remember, I have loved Him. It was just that during my third year in university something happened. There was a passion for Jesus I had not known before.

It was an invigorating time in my life filled with joy and newness of life. My fellow physics and math students could see it! Apparently it radiated from me—so much so that many asked if I could meet after class to explain why I was so alive.

In those afternoon and evening conversations my fellow students pressed me, and hard! They asked:

"Why Jesus?"

"Why love Jesus?"

"What is so special about Jesus?"

"What makes Jesus any more important than any other religious or philosophical figure?"

One day the professor who was teaching us thermodynamics (the study of heat and energy transfer) asked if he could meet with me! I was one of three or four students he had taken under his wing; he had been trying to get me a summer internship at the Institute of Plasma Physics in Berlin, Germany. I shared with him what was happening in me—that I was wrestling with a possibility of leaving physics to go to seminary and prepare for the preaching ministry. And he asked me—with all seriousness—"Why would you throw away your brains and your promising future to preach Jesus?"

Even then I knew there were a number of significant things that set Jesus apart. But thanks to my Sunday School upbringing, I knew there was one thing that put Jesus in a class all by Himself: Jesus of Nazareth, Son of Mary, is the Living God in human form. Jesus is the Creator become a creature. Or at least that is what the Church claims.

For centuries the Church has proclaimed that the God who made the world "came down" to live in the world as one of us. That claim is what generated the intense theological controversy of the first three or four centuries of Church history. That claim, and the attempt to unpack it, lies at the heart of all the so-called "ecumenical creeds." The Nicene Creed for instance, says of Jesus that He is, "God of God, Light of Light, very God of very God." The First Assembly of the World Council of Churches meeting in Amsterdam in 1948 found its unity in the affirmation, "Jesus Christ is Savior *and* God."

But the question haunted me. Did Jesus of Nazareth Himself ever make such a claim? Did He ever say that He is God?

So, along with textbooks on quantum mechanics and differential equations, I decided to read the New Testament with greater vigour. As I read, it appeared to me that the writers of the various New

Testament documents believed Jesus was Divinity in some form. The Apostle John says so right up front: "In the beginning was the Word, and the Word was with God, and the Word was God. And the Word became flesh and dwelt among us" (John 1:1, 14).

The Apostle Paul is just as forthright. As a science student, I was particularly drawn to his epistle to the Colossians. In it he says things like: "Christ is the image of the invisible God" (Col. 1:15). "For by Him all things were created" (1:16). "He is before all things and in Him all things hold together" (1:17). "In Him all the fullness of Deity dwells in bodily form" (2:9).

I was further taken by the fact that the writers of the New Testament gave to Jesus names and titles which only the God of the Old Testament had. For instance, they called Jesus "the Holy One" and "Lord."

As I read the New Testament, I saw that Jesus performs deeds which only the God of the Old Testament performs. Jesus forgives sins! Jesus raises the dead! Jesus stills the raging waters of the Sea of Galilee! And Jesus makes people's response to Him the basis of their eternal destination!

Furthermore, I noticed that Jesus was worshiped; He was given the kind of praise and adoration which only the Living God deserves. He gives sight to a blind man and the man worships Him. I was especially impressed by the fact that when doubting Thomas falls at the feet of the resurrected Jesus and cries out, "My Lord and my *God*," Jesus does not rebuke him (John 20:28). Jesus does not accuse him of the sins of idolatry or blasphemy. Jesus welcomes Thomas's worship!

But the question still haunted me. Did Jesus of Nazareth Himself, the Carpenter from Galilee, the flesh-and-blood human being whom other flesh-and-blood human beings touched, did He Himself ever say anything remotely like "I am the Living God"?

The question was intensified for me by the rock opera *Jesus Christ Superstar*. Now the question sang in my soul: *Jesus Christ, Superstar, Who are You? What do You say You are? Jesus Christ, Superstar, Who are You?*

This seemed to me to be so critical that I decided to re-read the four Gospels with that one question in mind.

To my good fortune I began with the Gospel according to John. I had learned in Sunday School that whereas Mark primarily focuses on Jesus's deeds, Matthew primarily emphasizes Jesus's teaching (especially about the Kingdom of God), and Luke is primarily concerned to establish the historicity of the Jesus story and show how Jesus did what He did and taught what He taught (that is, through prayer and the Holy Spirit), John's primary concern is Jesus's own self-understanding. More than the other three evangelists, John is interested in what the Nazarene has to say about Himself.

Now as I read and re-read John, I found myself especially intrigued with chapters seven and eight. When I made my way through those chapters I felt as if I should take off my shoes for I was on holy ground. In these chapters Jesus makes enormously audacious claims about Himself, claims that caused the religious authorities to finally ask Jesus, "Who are You?" (John 8:25) and "Whom do You make Yourself out to be?" (8:53).

I noticed that John is careful to tell us, his readers, that those enormous claims were made during the Jewish Feast of Tabernacles (7:2). I set out to get my hands on all the resources I could find to better understand this Feast. When I did, Jesus's words in John 7 and 8 came alive in me. I should say, they exploded in me! His words took on fresh meaning, and I found an answer to my question, which I offer you.

The Feast of Tabernacles

There were three Feasts which every male adult living within twenty-five kilometres of Jerusalem was obliged to attend: Passover, Pentecost and Tabernacles. Tabernacles was by far the most joyous. As mentioned previously, it was held in the fall, usually mid-October. Jerusalem overflowed with hundreds of thousands of very happy pilgrims. Those who came to the Feast would live in little huts or tents made of tree branches, which in Hebrew are called *sukkoth*. The worshipers did this as a way to recall the days when their ancestors lived in huts and tents as they made their way across the Sinai Desert from Egypt to the Promised Land.

The Feast of Tabernacles is extremely rich in symbolism and ritual and theology. There are three major components: a water ceremony, a light ceremony, and a fundamental theological affirmation that is recited in the festival liturgy.

The Water Ceremony

The water ceremony very dramatically recalls the fact that while traveling across the desert the ancestors found themselves without water. On one occasion God told Moses to go to a certain rock and strike it, promising that water would flow out of it. Moses did as commanded and, lo and behold, there was water in abundance! Rivers flowed! Water from a rock!

The Feast recalls that miracle and celebrates the fact that it was a sign of the greater miracle to come—the miracle of God pouring out of His Spirit upon His people, filling and flooding them with the water of life.

It is during this water ceremony on the last and greatest day of the Feast, says John, that Jesus cries out above the noisy crowd: "If you are thirsty, come to Me and drink; as the Scripture says, 'out of your innermost being will flow rivers of living water'" (7:37–38).

The Light Ceremony

As previously mentioned, the light ceremony, also very impressive, recalls the fact that while traveling across the desert the people did not lose their way. God guided them with a pillar of fire by night and a cloud of smoke by day.

The light ceremony celebrated the God who guides, the God who can guide because God is light. It is during the light ceremony that Jesus stands up and says, "I Am the Light of the *kosmos*. Anyone who follows Me will not walk in the darkness, but will have the Light of Life" (8:12).

The Festival Liturgy

Before we can listen to Jesus speak about Himself related to the fundamental theological affirmation celebrated in the festival liturgy, we need to understand the liturgy text in its first century context. As I said, those who came to the Feast of Tabernacles would live in little huts or tents made of tree branches. And as I said, the worshipers did this as a way to recall the days when their ancestors lived in little huts and tents while making their way to the Promised Land.

But the worshipers also did this as a way to recall that during those days the Living God chose to dwell among the people in a tent called the Tabernacle (hence the name Feast of Tabernacles). After the exodus from Egypt, God had commanded Moses to raise funds from the Israelites saying: "Let them construct a sanctuary for Me, that I may dwell among them" (Exod. 25:8).

Picture it: *"that I may dwell among them."* In Exodus we find this sanctuary, this Tabernacle, described to the smallest detail. It was to be the place where the Living God would meet the redeemed people. God says to Moses:

> "I will dwell among the [children] of Israel and will be their God. They shall know that I am the LORD their God who brought them

out of the land of Egypt, that I might dwell among them; I am the LORD their God. (Exod. 29:45–46)

Thus as Israel traveled across the Sinai Desert there was this glorious and abiding sense of the presence of God surrounding this Tent-Tabernacle.

Therefore, the central focus, the fundamental theological affirmation, of the Feast of Tabernacles is the *presence of the Living God*. The Feast celebrates God's gracious decision to dwell among His people and to manifest His glory to His people.

This fact was celebrated verbally throughout the festival liturgy. A number of Old Testament texts played a significant part in that liturgy. These Jewish Feasts all have their special liturgy. Just like we do. If you come to the Christmas Eve service, we are going to read from either Matthew 1–2 or Luke 1–2. You are not going to get Deuteronomy or 1 Corinthians 15 on the Resurrection. You are going to get a text prescribed for Christmas.

The Feast of Tabernacles also had prescribed texts. As we examine some of these texts, pay attention to how God is spoken of and how God speaks of Himself.

Deuteronomy 6:4, the fundamental creed of Israel: Hear, O Israel! The LORD is our God, the LORD is one!

Psalm 115:9–11 (emphasis added):

> O Israel, trust in the LORD—*He* is their help and their shield.
> O house of Aaron, trust in the LORD—*He* is their help and their shield.
> You who fear the LORD, trust in the LORD—*He* is their help and their shield.

Did you notice the recurring pronoun "He"? Three times: *He, He, He.*

Psalm 46, 50 and 81 were also sung during the feast. Note particularly Psalm 46:4–5, 10 (emphasis added):

> There is a river whose streams make glad the city of God,
>   the holy dwelling place of the Most High.
> God is in the midst of her, she will not be moved...
> "[Be still], and know that *I* am God;
>   *I* will be exalted among the nations,
>   *I* will be exalted in the earth."

Did you see the recurring pronoun "I"? Three times: *I, I, I.*

Of most significant importance were the portions of Isaiah 40–55 which were also read throughout the service.

Isaiah 41:4 (emphasis added):

> "I, the LORD, am the first, and with the last *I am He.*"

Isaiah 43:10 (emphasis added):

> "You are My witnesses," declares the LORD,
>   "and My servant whom I have chosen,
> So that you may know and believe Me
>   and understand that *I am He.*"

Isaiah 46:4 (literal translation emphasized):

> "Even to your old age [*I am He*],
>   And even to your graying years I will bear you!"

Did you catch the recurring combination of the pronouns "I" and "He" in the phrase "I am He"?

Divine Pronouns

Now, let me give a little foreign language lesson as we pay careful attention to the "I-He" pronouns in the festival liturgy.

The Hebrew word for "I" is *Ani*. The Hebrew word for "He" is *hu*. Therefore *Ani hu* literally means "I-He." In the Isaiah verses above, the phrase "I am He" was used to render *Ani hu*.[1] The implied verb "am" is inserted between the pronouns so that "I-He" in Hebrew makes sense in English.

When the Hebrew Old Testament was translated into Greek, the translators uniformly rendered *Ani hu* by the Greek words *ego eimi*. Ordinarily *ego eimi* would be translated "I, I am," or only "I AM." But because of the *Ani hu–ego eimi* connection, most translations rendered *ego eimi* as "I am He." This time the implied predicate "He" is inserted.[2] In this book I have chosen to foreground a more literal translation and will render *Ani hu* and *ego eimi* as "I Am He."

Here is the point of all this data. It is the single most important piece of data I can ever pass on to you. When we grasp it, we finally "hear" who Jesus thinks He is.

On the Sabbath of the Feast of Tabernacles the Levitical priests sang the so-called "Song of Moses" recorded in Deuteronomy 32. The high point of that song is verse 39 (emphasis added) where we hear God speak: "See now that *I, I am He*, And there is no god besides Me; It is I who put to death and give life."

The Hebrew is *Ani, Ani hu*. "I, I Am He." The Greek is *ego, ego eimi*. "I, I Am He." The divine pronouns.

According to the German scholar Ethelbert Stauffer, by the first century those little pronouns *Ani hu* or "I-He" had become "the all-inclusive summary of God's self-revelatory declarations in the ritual of the Feast of Tabernacles."[3]

The great Rabbi Hillel the Elder used to say in reference to this Feast, "When *Ani* is here, all is here. When *Ani* is not here, who then is here?"

At one point during the Feast, a choir of priests would sing at the altar, "God is in His Temple." Then, a priest singing God's Word would respond, "Be still and know that I am God." Then the choir of priests would chant again and again and again:

> *"Ani, Ani hu—Ani, Ani hu."*
> *"Ego, ego eimi—Ego, ego eimi,"*
> "I, I Am He—I, I Am He."

Thus, at the Feast of Tabernacles, along with the images of water and light, the words *"Ani, Ani hu," "Ego, ego eimi,"* "I, I Am, I Am He," were reverberating in the minds and hearts of the Jewish worshipers as they anticipated the real presence of the Creator. They were expecting that any moment now the Living God would show up!

Now we are ready to hear Jesus of Nazareth speak for Himself.

Who Jesus Claims to Be

John tells us that after Jesus made the claim, "I Am the Light of the world" (John 8:12), the religious authorities engaged Him in an intense debate. Jesus says that He will soon be going away and that they will search for Him and not find Him, and will end up dying in their sins. They discuss what all of this means.

Jesus says to them, "You are from below; I am from above. You are of this world; I am not of this world" (8:23). That in itself is a startling enough thing to say! Then Jesus says, "I told you that you would die in your sins; for you will die in your sins unless you believe that *I Am He*" (8:24).

Did you hear Him? "I–He, *ego eimi*." The authorities did—loud and clear! The Carpenter had just uttered those sacred pronouns of God's self-revelatory declaration during the Feast—and He uttered them in reference to Himself! That is why they ask Him, "Who are You?" They ask it in white-hot anger. "Who are you, Jesus? Come on man, You've got to finish the sentence. You can't leave it at 'I-He.'"

More debate ensues. Then Jesus says, "When you have lifted up the Son of Man." "Son of Man" was Jesus's favourite way of speaking of Himself; "lifted up" refers to His being lifted up on the cross to die. Jesus says, "When you lift up the Son of Man, then you will know that *I Am He*" (8:28).

Ego eimi. Ani hu. The very words by which Yahweh the Almighty, Yahweh the one and only, chooses to be known to Israel. And the Man from Galilee, the Son of Mary, dares to say, "Unless you believe that *I Am He* you will die in your sins." "When you have lifted Me up on the cross then you will realize that *I Am He*."

The debate understandably intensifies! Jesus is even accused of being possessed by a demon (8:48, 52). Toward the end of the argument Jesus says, "Your ancestor Abraham rejoiced that he would see My day, he saw it and was glad" (8:56). The authorities say to Him, probably with a cynical chuckle, "You are not yet fifty years old, and You have seen Abraham!" (8:57). Then Jesus drives home the magnitude of His Tabernacle claim. "I tell you the truth," Jesus answered, "Before Abraham was born, *I AM!*" (8:58). *Ego eimi, Ani hu!* Note, not "before Abraham was, I *was*" but "before Abraham was, I *AM*."

John tells us that immediately the authorities picked up stones to throw at Jesus. Why? Why throw stones at Jesus? Why throw stones at the gentle Carpenter? Why throw stones at a Man who heals you? Why throw stones at a Man who loves the way no one ever had loved? They had to. For right in the middle of the Feast that celebrates the Living God dwelling among His people, Jesus of Nazareth says, *"I AM HE!"*

A few months later, at the Feast of Dedication, or Hanukah, the authorities again take up stones to throw at Jesus. Jesus responds by saying, "I showed you many good works from My Father. For which of these are you stoning Me?" They answer, "For a good work we do not stone You, but for blasphemy; because You, a mere man, claim to be God" (10:32–33). That is precisely what the Carpenter had done at the Feast of Tabernacles.

Multiple Occasions of Jesus's Claim

Once I discovered this, my eyes and ears were opened to other times and places where Jesus made the same claim. Let me give you just a few illustrations also found in the Gospel of John.

John 4

In the fourth chapter of John, Jesus is talking with a Samaritan woman at a well. They are discussing worship. She wants to know where the proper place to worship is: on the mountain in Samaria or in Jerusalem? Jesus tells her that the place is not the issue. He says to her:

> An hour is coming, and now is, when the true worshipers will worship the Father in spirit and truth; for such people the Father seeks to be His worshipers. God is Spirit, and those who worship Him must worship in spirit and truth. (John 4:23–24)

The woman likes what she is hearing but she is not sure about Jesus so she says, "I know that Messiah (called Christ) is coming. When He comes, He will explain everything to us" (4:25). Then Jesus says to her, "I Am He (*ego eimi*), the One who is speaking to you" (4:26).

Is Jesus simply saying "I am the Messiah"? I do not think so. I think He is saying "I Am He." I think He is saying, "Woman, you need not go to another place, for *I Am He*, the very One you seek to worship."

John 6

In the sixth chapter of John we find Jesus, after feeding the 5,000, walking on the water. When the disciples first see Him they become very frightened (6:19). Then Jesus says to them, "I Am He (*ego eimi*); don't be afraid" (6:20). Is Jesus simply saying, "Hey guys, it's OK. Don't worry, it's me—Jesus"? I do not think so. They could see it was the Man they knew.

John is careful to tell us that this event took place during the Feast of Passover. During Passover one of the texts of Scripture read during that Feast was Isaiah 51:6–16. There, Isaiah recalls how God dried up the Red Sea so that the people could pass through, or as Isaiah puts it, "cross over" (51:10). The Isaiah text exalts Yahweh, the great "I Am He" (*ego eimi*) as Maker (51:12–13) and Lord over the sea (51:15).

You can see then that what Jesus is saying to His disciples is so much grander. He is saying, "You need not be afraid, I can control the seas, for *I Am He*."

John 18

In the eighteenth chapter of the Gospel of John we find these little pronouns again. But this time in a very solemn occasion in the Garden of Gethsemane. Judas the betrayer has come with the Roman battalion and with the officers of the Temple. John writes: So Jesus, knowing all the things that were coming upon Him, went forth and said to them, "Whom do you seek?" They answered Him, "Jesus the Nazarene." He said to them, "I am *He* (*ego eimi*)" (John 18:4–5).

Again, is Jesus simply saying, "You have found Him. I am the Nazarene"? No! And John makes that clear in the next verse: "When Jesus said, 'I am He,' they drew back and fell to the ground" (18:6).

Why? Why draw back and fall to the ground? Why fall to the ground before a Man they came to arrest? Were they taken by His courage? Were they overwhelmed with the moral innocence of the Man they came to throw in prison? Or were those Jews so accustomed to prostrating themselves immediately when they heard the divine pronouns, "I–He," that they responded without thinking?

Mark

I want to point out that John is not the only Gospel writer to record Jesus's use of God's self-revelatory pronouns. Mark records two instances where Jesus utters the words. The first is in Mark 6:50—the walking on water event we also looked at in John 6:20.

> Shortly before dawn, [Jesus] went out to them, walking on the lake. He was about to pass by them, but when they saw Him walking on the lake, they thought He was a ghost. They cried out, because they all saw Him and were terrified. Immediately He spoke to them and said, "Take courage! It is I (*ego eimi*). Don't be afraid." (Mark 6:48–50 TNIV)

The other is in Mark 14, during Jesus's trial before the Sanhedrin. The high priest asks, "Are you the Messiah, the Son of the Blessed One?" and Jesus replies, "I Am" (14:61–62). The Greek is *ego eimi*, the words we have been rendering as "I Am He." Mark tells us that the high priest tore his clothes saying, "Why do we need any more witnesses? You have heard the blasphemy. What do you think?" (14:63–64). The vote was unanimous. Jesus was guilty of using the divine pronouns in relation to Himself.

Given the strict monotheism of the first disciples and all the writers of the New Testament, you can imagine how Jesus's Tabernacle claim raised all kinds of serious theological struggles. John, Peter, Paul, and the author of Hebrews strain the Greek language, grasp for analogies, search for philosophical categories to express the totally unprecedented and unexpected. The wrestling continued way beyond the New Testament period. Council after Council met to try to come to terms with Jesus. Out of all the wrestling emerged the two mysteries at the centre of the Christian faith. According to J. I. Packer they are: the mystery of the plurality of Persons within the Godhead, leading to the doctrine of the Trinity; and the mystery of the unity of human and Divine in one person, leading to the doctrine of the Two Natures, to the fully God/fully human affirmation.[4]

Now you can dismiss that as theological mumbo-jumbo if you want, but what what Jesus said at the Feast of Tabernacles remains.

C. S. Lewis, the British scholar from Oxford, writes in his essay titled "What Are We to Make of Jesus Christ?" the following:

> If you had gone to Buddha and asked him, "Are you the Son of Brahman?" he would have said, "My son, you are still in the Vale of Illusion." If you had gone to Socrates and asked, "Are you Zeus?" he would have laughed at you. If you had gone to Mohammed and asked, "Are you Allah?" he would have first rent his clothes and then cut your head off. If you had asked Confucius, "Are you heaven?" I think he would have probably replied, "Remarks which are not in accordance with nature are in bad taste."[5]

But when the Temple authorities went to Jesus of Nazareth during the Feast of Tabernacles in AD 32 and asked, "Who do you make Yourself out to be?" Jesus replied, "Truly, truly, I say to you, before Abraham was born, *I Am*" (John 8:58). "When you lift up the Son of Man then you will realize that *I Am He*" (8:28). "Unless you believe that *I Am He* you will die in your sins" (8:24).

In Light of Who Jesus Claims He Is

The implications of all of this are literally endless—and staggering. Let me point to three.

(1) In light of Jesus's Tabernacle claim we now understand why He can make the other claims He makes. If He is "I Am He," the great "I AM," then of course He can say, "I Am the Bread of Life," "I Am the Resurrection and the Life," "I Am the Way, the Truth, and the Life." Of course He can say, "Let anyone who is thirsty come to Me and drink." Of course He can say, "I Am the Light of the world." Of course He can say, "I Am the Vine, you are the branches; abide in Me for apart from Me you can do nothing."

And of course He can say to us that He is absolutely necessary for human life. This Man is the very Ground of all our being. Without Him we simply cannot live!

(2) In light of Jesus's Tabernacle claim we can now appreciate why the rest of the New Testament puts Him at centre stage. We can see why the New Testament puts Jesus at the centre of everything! And we can understand why it is so critical what we decide what we are going to do with Him.

Given who He thinks He is, He has every right to walk into our lives, interrupt our plans and command us—*command us: "Come to Me. Follow Me. Lose your life for Me!"*

And given who He thinks He is, we are crazy not to obey! We are crazy not to come, not to follow, not to lose our lives for Him.

Given who He thinks He is, we see how *irrational*—I use this word deliberately—how just plain irrational it is for governments to operate without reference to Jesus. We see how irrational it is for corporations to operate without reference to Jesus. We see how irrational it is for universities to operate without reference to Jesus.

In light of His great Tabernacle claim we see why life is so miserable when we do not do it Jesus's way. The only *rational*, sensible, logical, truly realistic thing to do is surrender to the Centre of Life.

In the C. S. Lewis essay which I quoted earlier, Lewis observes that Jesus produced only three effects on those He met. They are hatred, terror and adoration. "There was no trace of people expressing mild approval."[6]

Mild approval? If Jesus is in fact who He thinks He is, then He is worthy of our impassioned worship. He is worthy of our impassioned love. He is worthy of our impassioned allegiance in every sector of life!

(3) In light of Jesus's Tabernacle claim we now understand why the Gospel of Jesus Christ is *the greatest news* anyone can ever hear. For what event stands at the heart of the Gospel? The crucifixion, right? Jesus lifted up! Jesus, arms out-stretched, hands nailed to the cross!

But who is this Jesus?

Who is this Man on the cross?

Whose arms are stretched out?

Whose hands are nailed to the wood?

Whose blood?—Whose blood is dripping to the ground?

In light of Jesus's Tabernacle claim, those arms are the arms of God! Those hands are the hands of God! Those bleeding wounds are the wounds of God!

It is *God* who suffers there!

It is the *Creator* who suffers there!

It is *I Am He* who becomes sin there!

It is the great *I AM* who takes upon Himself the just punishment for the sins of the world.

It is *I AM HE* who cries out, "*It is finished*!"

Everything that needs to be done about sin has been done. It is finished! Everything that needs to be done about my sin, your sin, has been done. *God is satisfied.* God is satisfied with the sacrifice of this Man because *this Man is God*!

In light of Jesus's Tabernacle claim, you can appreciate why my favourite hymn is Charles Wesley's "And Can It Be?"

> And can it be that I should gain
>   an interest in the Saviour's blood?
> Died He for me, who caused His pain,
>   for me who Him to death pursued?
> Amazing love, how can it be,
>   that Thou my God shouldst die for me?[7]

My God died for me? Yes! Yes! A thousand times—yes!

At one of the most sacred moments in the religious life of Israel, during the Feast of Tabernacles, when people were celebrating the presence of the Living God—the presence of the One who uses the pronouns *Ani hu,* "I–He"—it is *Jesus of Nazareth* who stands up and says: "Unless you believe that *I Am He* you will die in your sins." "When you lift up the Son of Man then you will know that *I Am He*." "Before Abraham was born, *I Am*."

That is why Thomas is not guilty of idolatry or blasphemy when he worships Jesus saying, "My Lord and my God."

And that is why I have not thrown away my brains to preach Jesus!

8

Listening to the Father Say Who Jesus Is

Hebrews 1:1–14

Who is He? Jesus: about whom we sing, in whose name we pray. Who is He?

We began by asking John the Baptist, the prophet sent by God to introduce Jesus to the world. Who does John think Jesus is? Of all that John has to say about his cousin, we focused on the claims, "the Lamb of God who takes away the sin of the world" (John 1:29) and "the One who baptizes in and with the Holy Spirit" (1:33).

We then talked to Jesus Himself. Who does He say He is? We heard Him claim to be "The Son of Man." Not just a son of man but *the* Son of Man, a title that put Him in a class all by Himself—no one else in world history ever dared to take to Himself that pretentious title. "You will see the Son of Man coming with the clouds of heaven" (Matt. 24:30).

We then heard Jesus claim: "I Am the Bread of Life—I am that without which you simply cannot live. You need Me more than your next meal" (John 6:48).

We heard Jesus claim: "I Am the Light of the world; whoever follows Me shall not walk in darkness but shall have the Light of life" (8:12). The Light that leads to life, the Light that *is* Life.

We heard Jesus claim to be the Stronger Man who invades the strong man's house, ties him up and begins to plunder his stolen property (Mark 3:27). Jesus claims to be stronger than all the forces that seek to undo the human race.

In the previous chapter we heard Jesus make the most astounding, most audacious claim anyone has ever made. We heard Jesus speak during the Jewish Feast of Tabernacles, during the Feast that celebrates the presence of the Holy God who promises to dwell among His people. We heard Jesus use the sacred pronouns of the Living God's self-revelation; we heard Jesus say, "I Am He." Jesus continues: "Unless you believe I Am He, you will die in your sins (8:24)." "When you have lifted up the Son of Man, then you will know I Am He" (8:28). "Before Abraham was born I AM" (8:58). I am still stunned by the implication of Jesus's claim! The world has felt very different since we examined this claim.

Listening to a Sermon, Hearing God's Voice

In this chapter let us listen to God say who Jesus is. More precisely, let us listen to God the Father say who He thinks Jesus is.

And where do we hear God speak of Jesus? In the New Testament document called "Hebrews." Notice how I put it? The New Testament document. I am not using the term "book." Although the document now comes to us in book form, it was not originally a book. Nor was it originally a letter. It was sent by mail, but it was not written as a letter for there is no letter-like introduction. The document simply launches in: "God, after He spoke . . . has spoken to us" (Heb. 1:1–2).

The document is a sermon—perhaps the most eloquent sermon ever written. The author says at the end of the document, "But I urge you, brothers and sisters, bear with this word of exhortation" (13:22). The word exhortation, *paraklesis*, is one of the words used for early Christian preaching. In Hebrews we have one of the most exquisitely crafted sermons ever preached! Some season, in years to come—unless the Son of Man should answer our prayers and come to all in His glory first!—I would like to take you through the whole sermon. "Bear with this word of exhortation for I have written to you briefly," says the author. Briefly? Thirteen chapters of dense theology—briefly?

It takes about seventy minutes to read through the sermon of Hebrews out loud. Seventy minutes is briefly?

In Hebrews we hear God say who He thinks Jesus is. Or again more precisely, we hear God the Father say who He thinks Jesus is. Even more precisely, we hear God the Father speak *about* and *to* Jesus.

Where? In the first chapter in Hebrews. The whole sermon begins: "God, after He spoke long ago to the ancestors in the prophets . . . in these last days has spoken to us in His Son (1:1–2). Literally just "in Son." "God has spoken in Son" and in chapter 1 we hear God the Father speak about and to Son.

Now, the author of Hebrews has so carefully crafted his sermon that chapter one cannot be separated form chapter two. A sermon is meant to be heard. Indeed, a sermon does not become a sermon until it is spoken. I handwrite my sermons on paper with pencil. And after writing I will often say to my wife Sharon, "I finished my sermon." Not so. The sermon on the pages of paper is not a sermon until it is spoken.

So too the sermon of Hebrews. It does not become what it is intended to be until spoken. It is meant to be heard. And it is when it is heard that it accomplishes its purpose. Furthermore, Hebrews 1–2 are meant to be heard together—neither chapter is finally heard without the other.

I now invite you, the reader, to experience the preaching of Hebrews 1–2.

Hearing Hebrews 1–2

(Hebrews 1–2 [TNIV] has been formatted to suggest a script for three speakers. The author of Hebrews is the preacher and follows the normal font. God's voice appears in upper case and Jesus speaks the italicized lines.)

In the past God spoke to our ancestors through the prophets at many times and in various ways, but in these last days He has spoken to us by His Son, whom He appointed heir of all things, and through whom also He made the universe. The Son is the radiance of God's glory and the exact representation of His being, sustaining all things by His powerful word. After He had provided purification for sins, He sat down at the right hand of the Majesty in heaven. So He became as much superior to the angels as the name He has inherited is superior to theirs.

For to which of the angels did God ever say,

"You ARE MY SON; TODAY I HAVE BECOME YOUR FATHER"?

Or again,

"I WILL BE HIS FATHER AND HE WILL BE MY SON"?

And again when God brings the firstborn into the world, He says,

"LET ALL GOD'S ANGELS WORSHIP HIM."

In speaking of the angels He says,

"HE MAKES HIS ANGELS SPIRITS, AND HIS SERVANTS FLAMES OF FIRE."

But about the Son He says,

"YOUR THRONE, O GOD, WILL LAST FOREVER AND EVER; A SCEPTRE OF JUSTICE WILL BE THE SCEPTRE OF YOUR KINGDOM. YOU HAVE LOVED RIGHTEOUSNESS AND HATED WICKEDNESS; THEREFORE GOD, YOUR GOD, HAS SET YOU ABOVE YOUR COMPANIONS BY ANOINTING YOU WITH THE OIL OF JOY."

He also says,

"IN THE BEGINNING, LORD, YOU LAID THE FOUNDATIONS OF THE EARTH, AND THE HEAVENS ARE THE WORK OF YOUR HANDS. THEY WILL PERISH, BUT YOU REMAIN; THEY WILL ALL WEAR OUT LIKE A GARMENT, YOU WILL ROLL THEM UP LIKE A ROBE; LIKE A GARMENT THEY WILL BE CHANGED. BUT YOU REMAIN THE SAME, AND YOUR YEARS WILL NEVER END."

To which of the angels did God ever say,

"SIT AT MY RIGHT HAND UNTIL I MAKE YOUR ENEMIES A FOOTSTOOL FOR YOUR FEET"?

Are not all angels ministering spirits sent to serve those who will inherit salvation?

We must pay the most careful attention, therefore, to what we have heard, so that we do not drift away. For since the message spoken through angels was binding, and every violation and disobedience received its just punishment, how shall we escape if we ignore so great a salvation? This salvation, which was first announced by the Lord, was confirmed to us by those who heard Him. God also testified to it by signs, wonders and various miracles, and by gifts of the Holy Spirit distributed according to His will.

It is not to angels that He has subjected the world to come, about which we are speaking. But there is a place where someone has testified:

> "What are mere mortals that you are mindful of them, human beings that you care for them? You made them a little lower than the angels; You crowned them with glory and honour and put everything under their feet."

In putting everything under them, God left nothing that is not subject to them. Yet at present we do not see everything subject to them. But we do see Jesus, who was made lower than the angels for a little while, now crowned with glory and honour because He suffered death, so that by the grace of God He might taste death for everyone.

In bringing many sons and daughters to glory, it was fitting that God, for whom and through whom everything exists, should make the pioneer of their salvation perfect through what He suffered. Both the One who makes people holy and those who are made holy are of the same family. So Jesus is not ashamed to call them brothers and sisters.

He says,

"I will declare Your name to My brothers and sisters; in the assembly I will sing Your praises."

And again,

"I will put My trust in Him."

And again He says,

"Here am I, and the children God has given Me."

Since the children have flesh and blood, He too shared in their humanity so that by His death He might break the power of him who holds the power of death—that is, the devil—and free those who all their lives were held in slavery by their fear of death. For surely it is not angels He helps, but Abraham's descendants. For this reason He had to be made like His brothers and sisters in every way, in order that He might become a merciful and faithful High Priest in service to God, and that He might make atonement for the sins of the people. Because He Himself suffered when He was tempted, He is able to help those who are being tempted.

❧

Wow.

And that is just the opening section of the sermon!

Did you hear the constant reference to angels? The term ties the two chapters together; the chapters begin and end with angels. "Angels" is an audio cue telling us that Hebrews 1–2 are meant to be heard together. Let's review all the references to angels:

1:4, "having become as much better than the angels"
1:5, "For to which of the angels did [God] ever say"
1:6, "Let all the angels worship Him"
1:7, "And of the angels He says,"
1:13, "but to which of the angels did He ever say"
1:14, "Are they not all ministering spirits (angels)"
2:2, "For if the word spoken through angels"
2:5, "For He did not subject to angels the world to come"
2:7, "You have made Him a little lower than the angels"
2:9, "We do see [Jesus] who was made for a little while lower than the angels"
2:16, "For assuredly He does not give help to angels"

Why all the references to angels? And what does this have to do with God the Father speaking about and to Jesus?

Mediators between God and Humanity

People of the first century lived in a universe filled with angels. So do we! It is just that they knew it. For people of the first century, Jews and Gentiles alike, angels served as the agents of communication between God and humanity. For them, angels were a kind of delivery service. It was thought that angels both brought God's word to humanity and brought humanity's word to God.

Imagine the diagram illustrating God up in heaven, humanity down on earth. It is thought that God mediated His relationship with human beings through angels. Angels carried Gods messages to humans and angels carried humanity's messages to God.

The author of Hebrews—the preacher—wants people to realize that although that view of the world may be true, in the coming of Jesus, things have changed. Although angels may still be around and still be useful to God and humans, "Are not all angels, ministering spirits, sent to serve those who inherit salvation?" (1:14). Nevertheless things have changed.

Jesus is now the mediator between God and humanity. Jesus is the one who brings God's word to humanity and who brings humanity's word to God. Jesus is the one who mediates God's and humanity's messages. Jesus is now the one sufficient mediator between God and humanity.

This is what being the high priest is all about. It is the dominant theme of the rest of Hebrews—Jesus the High Priest. The one final, sufficient Priest, surpassing and replacing all other orders of priests. Jesus the High Priest comes *from* the presence of God and brings us *into* the presence of God. Jesus is the only priest we need. Jesus is the only mediator we need. Thus, right at the beginning, the author of Hebrews preaches the good news. "Jesus has become as much superior to the angels as the name He has inherited is superior to theirs" (1:4).

Why? Why is Jesus the superior mediator? Why is Jesus more able to serve the role of mediator?

This question takes us to the heart of what the author of Hebrews is preaching in chapters one and two and the reason why the chapters need to be heard together. Jesus is the superior mediator because, unlike angels, Jesus knows both what it is like to be God and what it is like to be human. Jesus can mediate God to us because He knows God and knows what it is like to be God. Jesus can mediate us to God because He knows us and knows what it is like to be us. Jesus is the superior mediator because unlike angels, Jesus is both divine and human.

The Latin word for priest is *pontifex*. What is interesting to note is that *pontifex* is an engineering term. In particular a *pontifex* is a bridge builder. A priest is a bridge builder; a mediator is a bridge builder.

In order to build a bridge, the builder has to know both sides of the canyon over which the bridge is to be built, right? Jesus is the great Bridge Builder because He knows both sides of the canyon between God and humanity very well. He knows the divine side because He is divine and He knows the humanity side because He is human.

In the first chapter of Hebrews, the author, the preacher, demonstrates that Jesus is superior to the angels because He is God. In the second chapter of Hebrews (which we will attend to in the next sermon) he demonstrates that Jesus is superior to the angels because he is a man, the Man.

In Hebrews 1 the author makes a brilliant move. Instead of just stating the truth of who Jesus is, the author has *God* state the truth of who Jesus is. Brilliant. The author quotes a number of significant texts from the Old Testament in which the Living God speaks, texts with which his hearers would be familiar. And when the author of Hebrews quotes these texts, he quotes them as God speaking to Jesus. Somehow the Spirit of God who inspired the Old Testament texts enables this author of Hebrews to hear in the texts God the Father speaking to His Son. Brilliant, in every sense of the word.

So let us simply listen to God speak about and to Jesus. The author prepares us to hear what God is saying with a provocative rhetorical question.

To Which of the Angels Did God Ever Say . . . ?

"You Are My Son" (Heb. 1:5)

To which of the angels did God ever say what He says to Jesus? "You are My Son; today I have become your Father." Literally God says, "Today I have begotten You." We heard the Father say part of that text to Jesus at His baptism. As Jesus came up out of the water the voice from heaven said, "You are My Son whom I love" (Mark 1:11).

We hear the Father say it again at Jesus's transfiguration when Jesus is changed and He shines with the radiant glory of God. The Father says, "This is My Son whom I have chosen; listen to Him" (Luke 9:35). And now again in the sermon to the Hebrews the Father says what He has never said to angels or to anyone other would-be mediator: "You are My Son; today I have begotten You." A theologically loaded declaration!

The author of Hebrews hears God saying this to Jesus in the second Psalm. In Psalm 2 God declares that He has set His King on His holy mountain. The rulers of the world, in seeking to throw off any accountability to God, are engaged in futility for says God, "I have installed My King on My holy mountain" (Ps. 2:6). And then the king responds saying, "God said to me, 'You are My Son; today I have begotten you'" (2:7). And it goes on to say that God promised the Son all the nations of the earth as His inheritance (2:8).

Many scholars argue that Psalm 2 was read whenever a new king was installed in the life of Israel. That may be so. But what is certain is that the Psalm was read over a mere human king; everyone realized that no mere human king ever fit the bill. So for centuries the people of God realized that in Psalm 2 God was speaking of a king to come, of a Son to come, who would finally be God's King in the world.

The author of Hebrews hears what the Holy Spirit intends to be heard in Psalm 2; he hears God the Father speaking about and to Jesus. Jesus is the King who inherits all the nations of the earth because Jesus is the Son. "You are My Son."

"Today I Have Begotten You"

We continue to the next portion of the phrases God speaks in Hebrews 1:5. "Today I have begotten You." Many contemporary translations render it as "Today I have become your Father." OK, but the word the author of Hebrews uses is "*begotten*" which is a crucial word in the New Testament and particularly of Jesus. Although we do not, in modern English, use the word "begotten" anymore, we need to honour it in God's speech to Jesus.

"Begotten" versus "made." What we make *is not us*. What we make may be an expression of us—like a painting or a song, a quilt or a computer. Such things say something about who we are but they are not us. However, what we "beget" *is us* in some way. Not just an expression of us but us. Humans make automobiles and furniture. Humans beget babies. Humans beget humans.

So too with God. God makes all kinds of things: mountains, seas, giraffes, whales, hearts and brains and eyes and ears. But what God makes is not God. An expression of God, yes. Humans especially. "Let us make humans in our image" (Gen. 1:26). But we are not God. What God makes is not God.

What God begets is God! "You are My Son; today I have begotten You." His Son is not made, His Son is begotten. His Son is therefore not only just like God, He is God.

"Today I have begotten You." The "today" is *God's eternal today*. This is why the church creeds spoke of Jesus as "the eternally begotten Son." The creeds are wrestling with the claim, first made by a man names Arius, that Jesus the Son has not existed forever. As Arius put it, "there was a time when the Son was not," to which people like Athanasius responded, "Then there was a time when the Father was not a Father."[1] But the Father has existed as the Father from eternity and so has the Son. "Today." Eternally, forever, begotten—not made. And therefore eternally like the Father, God. "You are my eternally begotten Son."

"I Will Be His Father and He Will Be My Son"

Hebrews 1:5 again. To which of the angels did God ever say what He says to Jesus: "I will be His Father and He will be My Son"? The author of Hebrews hears the Father saying this in 2 Samuel 7. In that text, God is speaking to the Israelite King David, God's favourite earthly king. David has expressed his desire to build a beautiful temple for Yahweh. But Yahweh says, "No, you will not build it; but your son Solomon will." God says, "He will build a house for Me. I will be a father to him and he will be a son to Me" (2 Sam. 7:13–14).

Now, there is a sense in which Solomon lived in a father-son relationship with Yahweh. But as we read the Solomon story we realize that he did not even come close to what God intended in His promise. So, again, the people of God realize that God was speaking beyond David and Solomon and beyond all other mere human kings. The words to David about Solomon were clearly spoken about someone to come. And the author of Hebrews hears what the Holy Spirit intends to be heard in 2 Samuel 7; the author of Hebrews hears God the Father speaking about His only begotten Son. "I will be a Father to Him as He will be My Son."

And this is the key to understanding Jesus and His ministry. He lives His whole earthly life conscious that He is that unique Son of the Father. Again and again He speaks of being "the Son." One hundred times in the Gospel of John, for example. From the beginning of His earthly life to the end we hear Jesus say "Father." At the beginning, Jesus says to his mother and adopted father, "Did you not know I had to be about My Father's business?" (Luke 2:49). At the end, on the cross, "Father, into Your hands I commend my Spirit" (23:46).

Again and again we hear Him saying things like, "I only say what I hear the Father say," or "I only do what I see My Father do." As David Gooding of Ireland puts it: "No prophet, priest, poet, or king ever spoke of God as his personal Father in the way and to the extent that Jesus did."[2]

That is because no one else can. Jesus is the unique, only begotten Son of the Father. The wonder of the Gospel is that we who are made are adopted by the Father into that unique relationship—but this is another sermon!

"Let All the Angels Worship Him" (Heb. 1:6)

"When God brings His firstborn into the world"—when God brings His Son who is the principal heir of all things into the world—God says, "Let all the angels worship Him." Amazing! God, who alone is worthy of our worship, says about Jesus: "Let all the angels worship Him!"

The author of Hebrews is quoting Psalm 97. In that Psalm the psalmist is celebrating the sovereign reign of Yahweh. "Yahweh reigns; let the earth rejoice" (Ps. 97:1). Then, "Let all those be ashamed who serve graven images, who boast in idols" (97:7). And then the psalmist says, "Worship Him, all you gods" or "all you angels" (97:7). Worship Yahweh, not images of idols.

But the author of Hebrews hears something more; he hears what the Holy Spirit intends to be heard. The author hears not only a human being exhorting other human beings to worship Yahweh but Yahweh Himself exhorting the gods, the idols, to worship His Son! This is truly amazing!

One of the foundational themes of the whole Bible is that only God is to be worshiped. "You shall have no other gods before Me," is the first of the ten commandments (Exod. 20:3). "You shall worship the Lord your God and serve Him only," Jesus says to the devil in the wilderness (Matt. 4:10). When an angel gives the apostle John a vision of the new heaven and the new earth, John falls at the angel's feat to worship him. The angel is horrified and exclaims, "Do not do that; I am a fellow servant of Jesus. Worship God" (Rev. 22:8–9). And now we hear God the Father say that about Jesus His Son, "Worship Him. Let all the gods, all the angels, worship Him." The Father wants the angels and us to give His Son what the Father deserves. Worship Him. Worship My Son!

The Father has more to say about and to Jesus.

"Your Throne, O God!" (Heb. 1:8)

To which of the angels did God ever say what He says to Jesus— ready? "Your throne, O God, is forever and ever." *O God.* The Father says to Jesus, "O God." *Your throne, O God!* My goodness! That is why the Father exhorts us to worship Jesus. The Father addresses Jesus as God—*O God*. It takes my breath away!

The author of Hebrews is quoting Psalm 45 which is a love song celebrating the love between God's ideal king and his lover. Right in the middle of the story the psalmist exclaims, "Your throne, O God, is forever and ever" (Ps. 45:6). The psalmist is realizing that the ideal king will somehow sit on the throne of the universe. He is not addressing the king as God. He would never do that. But unknown to him, the psalmist is speaking beyond what he knows. The author of Hebrews hears that; he hears what the Holy Spirit intends to be heard. He hears God addressing His beloved Son: "Your throne, O God." Isn't this amazing?

This is why the author of Hebrews can say in the opening lines of his sermon that Jesus the Son is "the radiance of God's glory, the exact representation of God's nature" (Heb. 1:3). The word "radiance" means "shining forth." It is the property of light to shine forth; light radiates light. It is the property of God to shine forth; God radiates God. That radiation is Jesus the Light. "O God." The word "exact representation" refers to an image stamped on a coin. When you look at the image you see the character of the one in the image. When you look at Jesus you see who God is; you see the character of God. God the Father looks at Jesus and says "O God."

"O Lord!" (Heb. 1:10)

To which of the angels did God ever say what God says to Jesus? "In the beginning, O Lord, You laid the foundation of the earth." *O Lord, You. O Lord.* The Father addresses Jesus as "O Lord."

The author of Hebrews is quoting Psalm 102 which is a prayer for help in the face of decay and distress. The psalmist cries out, "Do not hide Your face from me in the day of distress" (Ps. 102:2). And in the middle of His prayer, he cries out, "But You, O Lord, abide forever" (102:12). And then, "In the beginning You laid the foundation of the earth" (102:25). "O Lord, You," is the cry of Psalm 102. O Lord, You. You remain forever. You remain the same. O Lord.

The Hebrew word for Lord is Yahweh, the sacred name of the God of Israel. *O Yahweh.* The psalmist calls out using this name. And the author of Hebrews hears in the psalmist cry the Father calling out to His Son, "O Yahweh." Yahweh calls out "O Yahweh." Yahweh calls Jesus "Yahweh"! *O Yahweh!*

"Jehovah" is the way the term was often rendered in the last centuries. *O Jehovah!* Jehovah calls Jesus "Jehovah"! *O Lord, O Jehovah, O Yahweh, You.* "You laid the foundation of the earth; the heavens are the work of your hands."

Which is why the author of Hebrews can say in the opening lines of his sermon that Jesus the Son is the One through whom God made the universe and Jesus the Son upholds all things by His powerful word (Heb. 1:3). Jesus made the world; Jesus upholds the world; Jesus made you; Jesus upholds you; Jesus made me; Jesus upholds me.

And always will. For as the Father says, "You, LORD, remain forever; everything else will change but You remain the same" (Heb. 1:12). Which is why the author of Hebrews can say the famous line: "Jesus Christ is the same yesterday, today and forever" (13:8). The author can say that because the Father says it. "O LORD, You remain the same forever."

"Sit at My Right Hand" (Heb. 1:13)

To which of the angels did God ever say what He says to Jesus? "Sit at My right hand until I make Your enemies a footstool for Your feet." The author of Hebrews is quoting Psalm 110:1. Psalm 110 is the text of the Old Testament that the New Testament quotes the most. Why? Because it speaks of Jesus as He is right now—seated at the right hand of the Father. The *right hand*; this is the symbol of authority. To sit at the right hand is to be invested with the authority of the one on the throne. The Father invests His Son with the Father's authority.

Sit. Jesus the Son has finished His crucial work for the Father, for us.

So the author of Hebrews ties chapters one and two of his sermon together by that great affirmation. "After He has provided purification for sins, He sat down as the Majesty of heaven" (Heb.1:3). "He made atonement for the sins of the people" (2:17). "Sit at My right hand," says God the Father to Jesus. "You have finished the work.

Sit, My Son. Sit, O God. Sit, O Yahweh. Sit, O Jesus. And one day all that opposes You and Your Kingdom will lie at Your feet."

And as the author of Hebrews can then say in the middle of his sermon: "The main point in what has been said is this: we have such a high priest who has taken His seat at the right hand of the throne of the Majesty in the heavens" (8:1). The one sufficient mediator between God and humanity has finished His crucial work and has taken His seat—the mediator of the new covenant, the mediator of a new agreement between God and humanity.

"Sit, My Son, My only begotten Son whom I have loved for all eternity."

Sit. O God, O Lord, O Jesus, sit.

9

Finally—A True Human

Hebrews 1–2

In Hebrews 1 and 2 we hear God speaking about and to Jesus! And we hear Jesus speaking about and to God! More precisely, in Hebrews 1 and 2 we hear God the Father speak about and to Jesus the Son and Jesus the Son speak about and to God the Father. Even more precisely, in light of what is revealed in Hebrews 1 and 2 we hear God the Father speak about and to God the Son *as one of us* and God the Son *as one of us* speak about and to God the Father.

So let us experience once again the opening section of the theologically and rhetorically exquisite sermon to the Hebrews. Note that there are three voices speaking to us: the author, God the Father and God the Son.

Hearing Hebrews 1–2

In the past God spoke to our ancestors through the prophets at many times and in various ways, but in these last days He has spoken to us by His Son, whom He appointed heir of all things, and through whom also He made the universe. The Son is the radiance of God's glory and the exact representation of His being, sustaining all things by His powerful word. After He had provided purification for sins, He sat down at the right hand of the Majesty in heaven. So He became as much superior to the angels as the name He has inherited is superior to theirs.

For to which of the angels did God ever say,

"You are My Son; today I have become Your Father"?

Or again,

"I will be His Father and He will be My Son"?

And again when God brings the firstborn into the world, He says,

"Let all God's angels worship Him."

In speaking of the angels He says,

"He makes His angels spirits, and His servants flames of fire."

But about the Son He says,

"Your throne, O god, will last forever and ever; a sceptre of justice will be the sceptre of Your kingdom. You have loved righteousness and hated wickedness; therefore God, Your God, has set You above Your companions by anointing You with the oil of joy."

He also says,

"In the beginning, LORD, You laid the foundations of the earth, and the heavens are the work of Your hands. They will perish, but You remain; they will all wear out like a garment, You will roll them up like a robe; like a garment they will be changed. But You remain the same, and Your years will never end."

To which of the angels did God ever say,

"SIT AT MY RIGHT HAND UNTIL I MAKE YOUR ENEMIES A FOOTSTOOL FOR YOUR FEET"?

Are not all angels ministering spirits sent to serve those who will inherit salvation?

We must pay the most careful attention, therefore, to what we have heard, so that we do not drift away. For since the message spoken through angels was binding, and every violation and disobedience received its just punishment, how shall we escape if we ignore so great a salvation? This salvation, which was first announced by the Lord, was confirmed to us by those who heard Him. God also testified to it by signs, wonders and various miracles, and by gifts of the Holy Spirit distributed according to His will.

It is not to angels that He has subjected the world to come, about which we are speaking. But there is a place where someone has testified:

> "What are mere mortals that you are mindful of them, human beings that you care for them? You made them a little lower than the angels; You crowned them with glory and honour and put everything under their feet."

In putting everything under them, God left nothing that is not subject to them. Yet at present we do not see everything subject to them. But we do see Jesus, who was made lower than the angels for a little while, now crowned with glory and honour because He suffered death, so that by the grace of God He might taste death for everyone.

In bringing many sons and daughters to glory, it was fitting that God, for whom and through whom everything exists, should make the pioneer of their salvation perfect through what He suffered. Both the One who makes people holy and those who are made holy are of the same family. So Jesus is not ashamed to call them brothers and sisters.

He says,

"I will declare Your name to My brothers and sisters; in the assembly I will sing Your praises."

And again,

"I will put My trust in Him."

And again He says,

"Here am I, and the children God has given Me."

Since the children have flesh and blood, He too shared in their humanity so that by His death He might break the power of him who holds the power of death—that is, the devil—and free those who all their lives were held in slavery by their fear of death. For surely it is not angels He helps, but Abraham's descendants. For this reason He had to be made like His brothers and sisters in every way, in order that He might become a merciful and faithful High Priest in service to God, and that He might make atonement for the sins of the people. Because He Himself suffered when He was tempted, He is able to help those who are being tempted.

 C₃

Who Is Jesus? The Superior Mediator

As we noted in the previous chapter, the people of the first century lived in a universe filled with angels. So do we! It is just that they knew it. For people of the first century angels served as the agents of communication between God and humanity; the angels were a kind of delivery service. It was thought that angels both brought God's word to humanity and brought humanity's word to God.

Imagine the diagram: God up in heaven, humanity down on earth. It was thought that God mediated His relationship with human beings through angels who carried God's messages to humans and human's messages to God.

The author of Hebrews wants people to realize that although that view of the world may be true, in the coming of Jesus things have changed. Jesus now mediates this relationship between God and humanity. Jesus is the One who brings God's word to humanity and who brings humanity's word to God. Jesus is the One who carries God's messages to humanity and carries humanity's messages to God. Jesus is the one final, sufficient mediator between God and man.

That is what being High Priest is all about. Jesus, the High Priest, comes to us from the presence of God and draws us into the presence of God. He is the only Priest who can do that. He is the only Priest we need. He is the only Mediator we need. So the author of Hebrews begins his sermon with good news.

In Hebrews 1:4 we read: Jesus has become "much superior to the angels." Superior? Why? Why is Jesus a superior mediator than the angels? Why is Jesus more able to serve the role of mediator? Answer? Jesus is the superior mediator because, unlike angels, Jesus knows both what it is like to be God and what it is like to be human. Jesus can mediate God to us because He knows God and knows what it is like to be God. Jesus can mediate us to God because He knows us and knows what it is like to be us.

As I also pointed out earlier, the Latin word for priest is *pontifex*. *Pontifex* is an engineering term referring to someone who builds bridges. A priest builds bridges. A mediator builds bridges. Now, in order to build a bridge, the builder has to know both sides of the canyon over which the bridge is to be built, right? Jesus is the great Bridge Builder because He knows both sides of the canyon very well! He knows the divine side because He is divine and He knows the human side because He is human.

Jesus is superior to the angels because, according to Hebrews 1, He is God. Jesus is superior to the angels because, according to Hebrews 2, He is a man, *the Man*.

Who Is Jesus? He Is God

Let me briefly review what God the Father says about and to Jesus the Son.

Hebrews 1:5: "You are My Son, today I have begotten You." Begotten, not made. Let me emphasize it again. Begotten, not made. What we humans make is not us. An expression of us, but not us. What we humans beget is us in some way. We make cell phones and rocket ships but we beget babies. Humans beget humans.

What God makes is not God. An expression of God, yes. "The heavens are telling the glory of God" (Ps. 19:1). But the heavens are not God. Neither are elephants or eagles or humans. What God makes is not God but what God begets is God. God begets God. "You are My Son . . . I have begotten You." Not just an expression of God, but God.

Hebrews 1:5 again. "I will be His Father, and He will be My Son." The most intimate relationship in the universe! And the Source of all other relationships.

Hebrews 1:6: "Let all God's angels worship Him." The Father is telling us that the urge we feel in the presence of Jesus of Nazareth, the urge to adore Him, is right. It is wholly appropriate; it is wholly Holy. When the magi come from the east and find Jesus in Bethlehem, they fall before Him—just an Infant!—and worship Him. Their hearts get it. "Worship My Son."

Hebrews 1:8: "Your throne, O God, is forever." *O God*. The Father addresses Jesus, "O God"!

Hebrews 1:10: "In the beginning, O LORD, You laid the foundations of the earth." The Father addresses Jesus, "O Lord"! The Father declares that the world in which He delights is the work of His Son. Jesus is the Creator of all things. "You, O LORD"!

Hebrews 1:13: "Sit at My right hand until I make Your enemies a footstool for Your feet." "Sit Jesus . . . sit, for Your work is done. Your death has accomplished all I said it would."

Who Is Jesus? He Is One of Us

Our purpose in Hebrews 2 is to listen to Jesus speak about and to God. Or more precisely, let us listen to God the Son *as one of us* speak about and to God the Father.

Notice how I have been putting it: "Listen to God the Son as one of us." As one of us—for that is what the author of Hebrews is emphasizing in chapter two of his sermon. One of us. He who is God—*O God*—becomes one of us! A human being. A real human being. A fully-human human being. Indeed, He becomes *the* human being. The *representative* human being. Not just "one of us" but He becomes *us*!

Before listening to Jesus speak about and to God the Father, let us take time to observe how the author of Hebrews demonstrates the real, full humanity of Jesus. It's rich! The text in Hebrews 2 is so rich, taking us deep into the mysteries of the Gospel.

Being Us: God's Design for Humanity

Hebrews 2:6–7

The author begins by quoting Psalm 8. "What is man that You are mindful of him, the son of man that You care for him?" (Ps. 8:4). The poet King David stands out under the starlit night sky and is awed by the fact that the awesome Maker of the stars recognizes and pays attention to us puny creatures on this small planet in the universe.

In Psalm 8 we have a biblical theology of humanity. God's original design if you will. The phrase "a little lower than the angels" in the Hebrew is literally "a little lower than God." The term is "Elohim," the plural form of the noun "El" which is the commonly used word for God. The Greek translation from which the author of Hebrews is quoting renders "elohim" not as God but as angels. Either way, the text is pointing to the greatness of us puny creatures!

Some of you may remember the television mini-series *Roots* about American slaves tracing their African ancestry. In one scene, in Kenya I think, a grandfather takes his newly born grandson in his hands, lifts him up toward the sky, points him to the God of heaven and says, "Behold! the only thing greater than you."[1] "A little lower than the angels."

"Crowned with glory and honour" (8:4). We were made to reflect the glory of God, made to reflect the nature and character of God. Crowned by God to be God's royalty. Princes and princesses in the Castle we were made to be. "Everything under their feet," says the Psalm (8:6). Created to rule with God in the world. Created as vice-regents. Created to run, and run in the Castle on behalf of the Great King.

Hebrews 2:8

The author of Hebrews adds "in putting everything under humans, God left nothing that is not subject to them." God's co-care-givers, co-workers in the Garden and in the Castle. Yet . . .

"Yet at present we do not see everything subject to humanity." A fact we all know and feel painfully: every time we think we have to go to war; every time an epidemic sweeps through a population; every time a drug dealer sells his poison; every time a woman's body is exploited on the Internet; every time a doctor says to us, "I cannot do anything more for you." In all those times we hear the "yet we do not see everything subject to humanity." We know something has gone wrong. Gone very wrong.

The French mathematician and philosopher Blaise Pascal was right: "All the miseries of man prove his grandeur; they are . . . the miseries of a dethroned monarch."[2] But . . .

Hebrews 2:9

"But we do see Jesus." In the midst of the Garden that has become a Cemetery, in the midst of the Castle that has been invaded by alien forces, we see one human being who is crowned with glory and honour.

God as One of Us—*How So?*

Now here is where reading Hebrews 1 and 2 together comes into play. According to Hebrews 1, who is this human of Hebrews 2? *It is God!* The human we see in the midst of all the wreckage is God. The man is God. "You shall call His name Immanuel, God with us," or more literally, the "with-us God" (Matt. 1:23).

"A little lower than the angels," says the author of Hebrews (2:9). Down where we are, with us, "lower than the angels." Amazing! He who made the angels and the stars, now lower than the angels and stars!

"Sharing our flesh and blood" (2:14), says the writer of Hebrews. "Like us in every way" (2:17). Not a phantom, but our flesh and blood.

"Tempted in every way as we are" (2:18), says the author of Hebrews. Tempted in our broken world not to believe. Tempted to live with the self at the center. Tempted to live an autonomous life. Tempted to live a self-directed life. Hungry. Thirsty. Tired. Lonely. Betrayed

by friends. Abused by enemies. Tempted and tested in every way we are. Indeed, to an even greater degree than we are!

God the Son, really one of us, really one *with* us. Immanuel, going through all the stages of physical, emotional, and mental development. As a twelve year old boy in trouble with His mother because He sought to live obedient to His Father. Later, all alone in the desert forty days without water, face to face with the evil that seeks to destroy everything God has made. Later, in the Garden of Gethsemane wrestling with what He must do but does not want to do, trembling at the consequences.

"Tempted in every way as we are." Says New Testament scholar Oscar Cullmann, "This is the boldest assertion of the complete humanity, the human character of Jesus, in the New Testament."[3]

"Tastes death for us," the author of Hebrews goes on to say. Hebrews 2:9 says, "so that by the grace of God He might taste death for everyone." For me this is the boldest assertion of the full humanity of the Son of God. "Taste death." The with-us God tastes death! It is what makes Jesus the perfect mediator. He really knows what it means to be us. He tastes what we taste all the time, all our lives. He tastes death.

Dorothy Sayers brings this out so meaningfully in her Christmas play, "He That Should Come." She has the three magi, the three wise men who have come across the desert from the east, express their hopes as they act out in response to the message of the star to find the newborn King. One of the magi, Balthazar, expresses the feeling of countless human beings:

> All I ask is the assurance that I am not alone,
>   some courage, some comfort against the burden
>   of fear and pain.
> About my palaces the jungle creeps and winds.
> Famine and plague are my fireside companions

and beyond the circle of the fire, the glare of human eyes.
Fear in the east, fear in the west,
>armies and banners marching and garments rolled in
>blood.
Yet this is nothing if only God will not be indifferent.
If He is beside me, bearing the weight of His own creation,
>if I may hear His voice among the voices of the vanquished,
>if I may feel His hand touch mine in the darkness,
>if I may look upon the hidden face of God
>and read in the eyes of God
>that He is acquainted with grief."[4]

In Hebrews 2, we see that the God of Hebrews 1 is acquainted with grief. As one of us He tastes death. As one of us God tastes death. In the eyes of Jesus I see that God knows grief. And because He has tasted death, He is perfected. (This is a mystery.)

"Made perfect through suffering." Jesus, "the author of their (our) salvation is made perfect through suffering" (2:10), that is, through tasting death. So fully human, so truly us, that He matures into His "fully mature humanity" through what He suffers in our broken world. A great mystery. Jesus the Son—so fully human, so truly us—like all humans, He grows into His full maturity.

Like a seed. A seed may be perfect as a seed, but it is not yet what it is intended to be until it grows out of its "seedness." It grows by dying, by giving up its life to the ground. God the Son, so completely human He *becomes* what He is intended to be through suffering.

God as One of Us—*Why?*

Why does He do it? Why does "He who is God" become a real, fully-human human?

"To render powerless the one who holds the power of death" (2:14), says the author of Hebrews. The Son enters into death. He tastes

death to de-fang death. Another mystery! Jesus conquers death "not by avoiding it or commanding it to disappear but by experiencing it."[5] The One who is God enters the devil's realm, tastes death, swallows death, and thereby conquers it. By giving Himself over to the power of death, He renders it powerless. Every Easter it seems, I quote the Welsh preacher Peter Joshua who said, "When death stung Jesus Christ it stung itself to death."[6] By death He conquers death.

And thus Jesus steals the enemy's chief weapon: the fear of death.

God the Son becomes fully us *"to deliver those who through the fear of death were subject to fear all their lives,"* says the preacher (2:15). Or "to free those who all their lives were held in slavery by their fear of death" (NIV). By conquering death through dying our death, Jesus sets us free from the "emotion that distorts our existence."[7] Jesus sets us free from the fear of non-being and therefore from all the ways we try to stave off non-being. Death no longer has the finality it once had.

All of this is made possible, says the author of Hebrews, because God the Son, as one of us, deals with the problem of sin that brought death into being in the first place. He becomes *us*, becomes fully human, to atone for sin, to give Himself as the final sacrifice that takes away the barrier sin erects between us and God. He becomes the merciful High Priest, the faithful High Priest, who *at once* is the One who offers the sacrifice and is the sacrifice *itself* (which is the great theme of the rest of Hebrews).

"Bringing many sons and daughters to glory" (2:10). Jesus does it all to bring us to glory. He is the Pioneer of our salvation, out front, clearing the way, leading us into the fullness of our salvation which is "glory." We were originally created to reflect the glory, to reflect the nature and character of God. And God the Son, as one of us, is bringing us back into that original design.

Which is why He is not ashamed to call us brothers and sisters. Hebrews 2:11 says, "Jesus is not ashamed to call them"—broken human beings—"brothers and sisters." Talk about granting dignity! The most perfect human being who ever lived, God in our flesh and blood, is not ashamed to stand before the watching world and point to us and say, "My brothers and sisters." We might be ashamed to do that. Are there not times when we are ashamed to say of one another in our brokenness "brother and sister"? Not the God-Man! He is not ashamed; He is not ashamed of you or me.

"This man welcomes sinners and eats with them," say the Pharisees (Luke 15:2). The word "welcome" means "as members of His family." They speak out in disgust, "This man, this Jesus, this so-called Holy One welcomes sinners. This Man eats with sinners (how disgusting!) and welcomes them into His family (disgusting!), tarnishing the reputation of the Holy God." "Not so," says Jesus, "not tarnishing the reputation of Holy God—honouring the reputation of Holy God." This is the reputation the Holy God wants to have in the city. "This Man eats with sinners and welcomes them." Jesus is not ashamed to call us brothers and sisters.

Hebrews 2: Hearing Him as One of Us

And now we hear Him speak, now we hear God the Son as one of us speak about and to God the Father.

Hebrews 2:12: *"I will declare Your Name to my brothers and sisters; in the congregation, I will declare Your Name."*

It is the driving force of the whole of Jesus's earthly ministry. He lives and dies to announce and to reveal the Name of His Father. "Name" is a way of saying nature or character. In the first century, if you knew someone's name, you knew something about the person's nature and character. Jesus lives and dies to make His Father's nature and character known to the world. Jesus lives and dies to show us who the Father is and what the Father is like. As He prays in His great High Priest prayer recorded in John 17, "I have made Your Name known and will continue to make it known." It is the deepest desire of God the Son's heart.

"I will declare." "I will announce." The term the author of Hebrews uses is another word the early Church used for its preaching. "I will preach," says God the Son as one of us. In saying, "I will preach," Jesus is revealing one of the mysteries of this moment and of every preaching moment.

When a preacher steps forward to preach the Name, he or she does not stand alone; he or she stands with the great Preacher. In every preaching moment Jesus Himself is preaching. All preaching participates in His preaching. It is because Jesus is preaching (at this very moment) that our souls are stirred, our spirits are lifted, our minds are changed. Hear the Son say to His Father, "I will preach Your Name" among my brothers and sisters.

Hebrews 2:12 again: *"In the presence of the congregation I will sing Your praises."*

Of course! Given what the Son knows about His Father, given the love the Son has for His Father, of course He sings the Father's praises. Jesus sings! Sings to His Father among the brothers and sisters in the congregation.

Wouldn't you like to hear Him sing? What a thrill that would be! To hear the only begotten Son sing His heart out to His Father! What would He sing? Would that someone could write the songs Jesus would sing.

Would sing? I should say *is singing*—the songs the Son is singing. For here we have another mystery of this moment and every moment of worship. When we sing our praises we are not singing alone. Yes, we are singing with one another. But the mystery is we are singing with Jesus! He is the great Worshiper in the congregation. Just as the

Father exhorts angels and us to worship His Son, so the Son invites us to join Him as He worships His Father. Hear the Son say to His Father, "I will sing Your praises in the congregation."

Hebrews 2:13: *"I will put My trust in Him."*

To trust God is the greatest act of worship. To trust the Father is the greatest response that we can give to the revelation of the Father. The Father deserves trust. Given who He is, He deserves the trust of humanity. In every circumstance. At every moment. Not to trust is a huge affront to His glory. Not to trust is to say, "You are really not as good as You claim to be; You are not as faithful, merciful, powerful as You claim to be." Trust is the highest form of worship.

Do we trust? Do you trust! Do I trust the Father as He deserves to be trusted? No. I do not. I try to give the trust God deserves but I can't. But Jesus does! This Man does. The God-Man does. He who is us trusts on our behalf. He believes on our behalf. He believes for us!

So who is Jesus? As one of us, Jesus is the great Preacher. He is the great Worshiper. And He is the great Believer. The Son of God as one of us gives the Father all the honour, worship and trust the Father deserves!

And one more word from the Son to the Father.

Hebrews 2:13: *"Here I am, and the children God has given Me."*

"The children God has given Me." Jesus sees us as gifts! Jesus sees us as the presents the Father gives Him! Jesus is the Father's gift to us and we are the Father's gift to Jesus! We are gifts! Jesus says to the Father, "Here I am—and all the children You have given Me."

Here I am.

Here I am.

Here I am.

Do you hear what Jesus is saying? Those steeped in the Bible, in the Old Testament, as the author of Hebrews, would have heard loud and clear. "Here I am." The Father is finally getting an answer to the very first question He asked humanity. In the Garden, in the Garden which had become a Cemetery because of the sin of Adam and Eve, in the castle where the princes and princesses had rebelled, God calls out, "Where are you?" And the humans hid from God, afraid to come out from behind the trees. "Where are you?"

"Here I am." "Here I am," says the representative human. "Here I am," says God the Son as one of us. "Here I am," says the One who is us! "Here I am—and all the children You have given Me."

That is the Gospel of Hebrews 1 and 2. God so loves humanity that He becomes humanity. God so loves us that He becomes us. God has not given up on His original design. The Living God so wants us to be all He wants us to be that He *becomes* all He wants us to be!

"Here I am." Finally.

"Here I am." The true human.

God the true human!

And that, brothers and sisters, is why we are drawn like a magnet to Jesus of Nazareth. That is why we find Him irresistible. Who is Jesus? He is everything we were meant to be. He is everything we long to be.

To Him be all the praise and glory now and forever more. Amen.

Notes

Chapter 1 The Lamb of God Who Takes Away the Sin of the World

1. Isaac Watts, "Join All the Glorious Names" (1709).

2. Leon Morris, *The Apostolic Preaching of the Cross* (London: Tyndale, 1965), 129.

3. Thomas Oden, *Guilt Free* (Nashville: Abingdon, 1980), 126.

4. Keith Miller, *Sin: Overcoming the Ultimate Deadly Addiction* (New York: HarperCollins, 1987), 27.

5. Ibid., 52.

6. To which a voice in the pew said, "No way!" as if on cue.

7. Miller, *Sin*, 54–55.

8. Joachim Jeremias in Gerhard Kittel, ed., *Theological Dictionary of the New Testament* (Grand Rapids: Eerdmans, 1964), 1:185–86.

9. Raymond E. Brown, *The Gospel According to John* (New York, Doubleday, 1966), 1:59. See also 1 Enoch 90:9–12.

10. Ibid., 81.

11. Ibid., 62.

12. Herman Waetjen, *A Re-ordering of Power: A Socio-political Reading of Mark's Gospel* (Minneapolis: Fortress, 1989), 236.

13. Morris, *Apostolic Preaching*, 141.

14. Alan Richardson, *An Introduction to the Theology of the New Testament* (New York: Continuum, 1958), 228.

15. Morris, *Apostolic Preaching*, 143.

16. Charlotte Elliot, "Just As I Am" (1835).

Chapter 2 The One Who Baptizes in and with the Holy Spirit

1. John Stott, *Baptism and Fullness: The Work of the Holy Spirit Today* (Downers Grove, IL: InterVarsity, 1975), 25.

2. Thomas A. Smail, *Reflected Glory: The Spirit in Christ and Christians* (London: Hodder and Stoughton, 1975), 153.

3. J. Rodman Williams, from an unpublished paper.

4. Dallas Willard, *The Divine Conspiracy: Rediscovering Our Hidden Life in God* (New York: HarperCollins, 1998).

5. George Croly, "Spirit of God, Descend upon My Heart" (1854).

6. Michael Cassidy, *Bursting the Wineskins* (London: Hodder & Stoughton, 1983), 122.

7. Michael Green, *I Believe in the Holy Spirit* (Grand Rapids: Eerdmans, 2004).

8. William Barclay, *The Gospel of Matthew* (Louisville: Westminster John Knox, 1975), 1:49.

Chapter 3 The Son of Man

1. Oscar Cullmann, *The Christology of the New Testament*, trans. Shirley Guthrie and Charles Hall (Philadelphia: Westminster, 1963), 155. See also F. F. Bruce, *Tradition Old and New* (Grand Rapids: Zondervan, 1970), 51–52, and I. Howard Marshall, *The Origins of New Testament Christology* (Downers Grove, IL: InterVarsity, 1976), 72.

2. Irenaeus, *Against Heresies* 3.19.

3. Author unknown, "Fairest Lord Jesus" (1677), stanza 1, "O Thou of God and man the Son," and stanza 4, "Beautiful Saviour, Lord of all the nations! Son of God and Son of Man!"

4. See Eugene Peterson, *Reversed Thunder: The Revelation of John and the Praying Imagination* (San Francisco: Harper & Row, 1988).

5. Carsten Colpe, *Theological Dictionary of the New Testament* (Grand Rapids: Eerdmans, 1974), 8:420.

6. George E. Ladd, *A Theology of the New Testament*, rev. ed. (Grand Rapids: Eerdmans, 1993), 156.

7. Ethelbert Stauffer, *New Testament Theology* (London: SCM, 1955), 19.

8. I heard this anecdote in a sermon that was part of a conference I was attending in Chicago.

Chapter 4 The Bread of Life

1. In Greek this is *ego eimi,* which commonly appears as "I am" for the sake of clarity in English. In this book I have chosen to render it as "I Am" to foreground a more literal translation. I develop this concept in chapter 7 ("I Am He").

2. Barclay, *Gospel of John*, 1:215.

3. Lesslie Newbigin, *The Light Has Come: An Exposition of the Fourth Gospel* (Grand Rapids: Eerdmans, 1982), 78.

4. Barclay, *Gospel of John*, 1:216.

Chapter 5 The Light of the World

1. Tim Hughes, "Here I am to Worship" (2001).

2. See *Sukkoth* 5:2–4.

3. Barclay, *Gospel of John*, 1:13.

4. Newbigin, *Light Has Come*, 102.

5. E. Stanley Jones, *The Word Became Flesh* (Nashville: Abingdon, 1968).

6. Ibid.

7. Cited in Ray C. Stedman, *Spiritual Warfare* (Grand Rapids: Discovery House, 1975), 20–21.

8. Newbigin, *Light Has Come*, 200. The term "disciple" in this quote has been altered to the plural form.

9. Henry J. van Dyke, "Joyful, Joyful, We Adore Thee" (1907).

Chapter 6 The Stronger Man

1. Martin Luther, "A Mighty Fortress Is Our God" (1853).

2. Adolf von Harnack, quoted in Robert H. Stein, *Mark*, Baker Exegetical Commentary on the New Testament (Grand Rapids: Baker Academic, 2008), 33.

3. James Dunn, "Demon Possession and Exorcism in the New Testament," in *Christ and the Spirit: Collected Essays by James D. G. Dunn* (Grand Rapids: Eerdmans, 1997), 2:216.

4. Bob Whitaker, friend and mentor, from a personal conversation.

5. C. S. Lewis, *Mere Christianity* (New York: HarperCollins, 1980), 160.

6. John White, *The Fight* (Downers Grove, IL: InterVarsity, 1976), 77–78.

7. James W. Sire, *The Universe Next Door: A Basic Worldview Catalog*, 4th ed. (Downers Grove, IL: InterVarsity, 2004), 18.

8. N. T. Wright, *Jesus and the Victory of God* (Minneapolis: Fortress, 1996), 138.

9. C. S. Lewis, *The Screwtape Letters* (New York: HarperCollins, 1941), vii.

10. Benjamin Britten, "This Little Babe" from *Ceremony of Carols* (1942).

11. Peter Andrew Furler, "He Reigns" (2003).

12. Luther, "A Mighty Fortress Is Our God" (1853).

Chapter 7 "I Am He"

1. A more accurate representation would be "I [am] He."

2. A more precise English rendering would be "I Am [He]." The NASB version denotes inclusions of implied words with italics (rather than square brackets). See, for example, John 18:4–5, quoted later in this sermon.

3. Ethelbert Stauffer, *Jesus and His Story* (London: SCM, 1960), 177.

4. J. I. Packer, *Knowing God* (Downers Grove, IL: InterVarsity, 1993).

5. C. S. Lewis, "What Are We to Make of Jesus Christ?" in *God in the Dock: Essays on Theology and Ethics* (Grand Rapids: Eerdmans, 1994), 157–58.

6. Ibid., 158.

7. Charles Wesley, "And Can It Be?" (1738).

Chapter 8 Listening to the Father Say Who Jesus Is

1. The Athanasian Creed of the sixth century was the first creed to assert the equality of the three Persons of the Trinity. This creed also refutes those who disagree with the creed.

2. David Gooding, *An Unshakable Kingdom: Letter to the Hebrews for Today* (Grand Rapids: Eerdmans, 1989), 56.

Chapter 9 Finally—A True Human

1. Alex Haley, *Roots* (1977).

2. Blaise Pascal, *Thoughts on Religion and Philosophy* (Glasgow: William Collins, 1838), 53.

3. Cullmann, *Christology of the New Testament*, 204.

4. Dorothy Sayers, "He That Should Come" (1939).

5. Luke Timothy Johnson, *Hebrews: A Commentary* (Louisville: Westminster John Knox, 2006), 100.

6. Peter Joshua, a dear mentor.

7. Johnson, *Hebrews*, 100.

CPSIA information can be obtained
at www.ICGtesting.com
Printed in the USA
LVHW102010140123
736969LV00004B/735